Excel 4 for Windc
SmartStart

Ralph Duffy
North Seattle Community College

Sharel McVey

College

Publisher: David P. Ewing

Associate Publisher: Rick Ranucci

Product Development Manager: Thomas A. Bennett

Operations Manager: Sheila Cunningham

Book Designer: Scott Cook

Production Team: Christine Cook, Lisa Daugherty, Brook Farling, Carla Hall-Batton, Caroline Roop, Sandra Shay, Tina Trettin

About the Authors

Ralph Duffy holds a B.A. from the University of Michigan and an M.S. from Pennsylvania State University. He has worked as a statistical consultant and programmer/analyst for Pennsylvania State University, the Indiana University School of Medicine, and Purdue University. He is currently an instructor in the Computer Information Systems Department of North Seattle Community College.

Mr. Duffy also is the Director of the IBM Technology Transfer Center in Seattle. This Center, in cooperation with Microsoft Corporation, provides training in computer applications for the faculty and staff of colleges throughout the Northwest, including the University of Washington and Seattle University.

Sharel McVey founded San Francisco Computer Services to provide software consulting and training services to companies, individuals, and trainers. Ms. McVey authored Que's *Excel 4 for Windows QuickStart*, *Excel 3 for Windows QuickStart*, and *Excel for Windows Quick Reference*. She holds a B.A. in Economics from San Francisco State University.

Title Manager
Carol Crowell

Senior Editor
Jeannine Freudenberger

Editor
Pamela Wampler

Editorial Assistant
Elizabeth D. Brown

Formatter
Jill Stanley

Trademarks

Composed in Garamond and MCPdigital by Que Corporation

Give Your Computer Students
a SmartStart on the Latest
Computer Applications

Que's SmartStart series from Prentice Hall Computer Publishing combines the experience of the Number 1 computer book publisher in the industry with the pedagogy you have come to expect in a textbook.

SmartStarts cover just the basics in a format filled with step-by-step instructions and screen shots.

Each SmartStart chapter ends with a "Testing Your Knowledge" section that includes true/false, multiple choice, and fill-in-the-blank questions; two or three short projects; and two long projects. The long projects are continued through the book to help students build on skills learned in preceding chapters.

Each SmartStart comes with an instructor's manual featuring additional test questions, troubleshooting tips, and additional exercises. This manual will be available both on disk and bound.

Look for the following additional SmartStarts:

Word for Windows SmartStart	1-56529-204-9
Windows 3.1 SmartStart	1-56529-203-0
MS-DOS 5.0 SmartStart	1-56529-249-9
WordPerfect 5.1 SmartStart	1-56529-246-4
Lotus 1-2-3 SmartStart (covers 2.4 and below)	1-56529-245-6
dBASE IV SmartStart	1-56529-251-0

For more information call:

1-800-428-5331

or contact your local Prentice Hall College Representative

Contents at a Glance

Table of Contents

Introduction

Microsoft Excel 4.0 is a popular and powerful spreadsheet application. You can use Excel to organize and analyze data, perform numerical calculations, and illustrate relationships in numerical data by displaying charts. Whether you are new to Excel or are upgrading to version 4.0 from an earlier version of Excel, this SmartStart tutorial provides you with the necessary, step-by-step information you need to use Excel.

If you are experienced with Windows, you may be familiar with many of the concepts used in Excel for Windows. If you are new to Windows, you will discover that Windows is a much easier and more intuitive operating environment than the traditional character-based environment.

All aspects of Excel 4.0 contain improvements, including enhanced analytical capabilities, greater flexibility with database management, increased charting options, and the capability to automate tasks and customize Excel with macros. Excel 4.0 also includes many new features designed to enhance its presentation capabilities. All Excel features focus on ease of use and increased productivity—which is why Excel is considered the spreadsheet of choice by many users.

Who Should Use This Book?

Excel 4 for Windows SmartStart is a tutorial developed with easy-to-follow, step-by-step instructions. Because *Excel 4 for Windows SmartStart* concisely covers only the most important concepts, your time on the learning curve is greatly reduced. Each chapter begins with a set of clear objectives. Each explanation of an Excel feature is followed by an exercise for you to perform using Excel on your computer. These exercises will reinforce your understanding of the concepts covered in the chapter. Projects and questions at the end of a chapter give you a chance to practice what you have learned and to check your understanding of the objectives.

How This Book Is Organized

Each chapter follows the same format. First, the chapter overview introduces the topics discussed in the chapter, and provides a clear list of chapter objectives. Next, key terms used in the chapter are defined. The body of the chapter presents step-by-step procedures that guide you through the required actions, and includes exercises that check for your mastery of the chapter objectives. Finally, each chapter ends with chapter review questions and projects.

The early chapters provide an understanding of Excel worksheet basics. The rest of the chapters discuss more advanced features, including functions, charting, and database management.

Chapter 1, "An Overview of Excel 4.0," explains the main components of Excel.

Chapter 2, "Getting Started," covers how to start Windows and Excel, and reviews the basics of the screen, menus, keyboard, commands, and on-line Help.

Chapter 3, "Excel Worksheet Basics," has you create an actual worksheet, teaches the basic skills required for working on a worksheet, including entering, editing, and selecting data; moving around the worksheet; accessing commands; saving files; and printing your worksheet.

Chapter 4, "Building a Worksheet," covers ranges; inserting, deleting, and copying; and changing column width and row height.

Chapter 5, "Formatting a Worksheet," shows you how to use Excel's various formatting commands to enhance the appearance of your worksheets. This chapter also explains how to use the Spelling Checker on your worksheet.

Chapter 6, "Using Functions," describes many of Excel's built-in functions and explains the types of functions used for a variety of business and scientific calculations.

Chapter 7, "Printing a Worksheet," covers all aspects of printing Excel worksheets, including setting the print area, printing headers and footers, page setup, orientation, and print preview.

Chapter 8, "Charting Data," teaches you the basics of creating a chart, changing a chart type, enhancing a chart, and printing a chart.

Chapter 9, "Managing Data," introduces the components of a database. This chapter also reviews how to create, edit, and sort a database and how to find and extract records that meet defined criteria.

The book concludes with the Appendix, "Summary of Excel 4.0 for Windows Commands," and a comprehensive index.

Where To Find More Help

After you have learned the Excel basics covered in the Excel SmartStart, you may want to explore some of the more advanced features of Excel 4.0. These features include linking worksheets, using add-ins, outlining, advanced charting, macros, creating custom dialog boxes with the Dialog Editor, and using Q+E for accessing external databases.

Que Corporation has a complete line of Excel books designed to meet the needs of all computer users. Other Excel books include *Using Excel 4 for Windows*, Special Edition, and *Excel 4 for Windows Quick Reference*. For more information about Que products, contact Que Corporation at 1-800-428-5331 (outside Indiana). In Indiana, call 1-317-573-2500.

Conventions Used in This Book

As with all Windows applications, you can use the mouse, the keyboard, or shortcut keys for most operations. Throughout the chapters, mouse and keyboard techniques are provided.

When a key or key combination appears in a procedure, keyboard character icons are used:

Combination	Keystroke
Alt, R	Press the Alt key, release it, and then press the R key.
Ctrl + F6	Hold down the Ctrl key, press the F6 function key, and then release both keys.

In this book, a key combination is joined by a comma or a plus sign (+):

Combination	Keystroke
Alt, **letter**	Press the Alt key, release it, and then press the underlined letter key.
Alt + **letter**	Hold down the Alt key, press the letter key, and then release both keys.

When you use the mouse to operate Excel, you will usually perform one of the following actions:

Action	Technique
Click	Place the mouse pointer on the item you want to select, and click the left mouse button.
Double-click	Place the mouse pointer on the item you want to select, and click the left mouse button twice in rapid succession.
Drag	Place the mouse pointer on the item you want to select, and hold down the left mouse button as you move the mouse.
Ctrl+Drag	Hold down the Ctrl key as you drag with the mouse.

This book uses the following special typefaces:

Typeface	Meaning
Italic type	This font is used for words or phrases defined for the first time, and for optional items in functions.
Blue, Boldface type	This font is used for user input—what you type, such as commands and functions. In a numbered list of steps, this font also indicates the keys you press to access menus and commands—File Open, for example.
Special font	This font is used to represent system and screen messages.

System Requirements for Running Excel 4.0

To provide optimum performance for Excel, your computer and software should meet or exceed the following requirements:

Hardware Requirements

- IBM or compatible computer with a hard disk and an 80286, 80386, or 80486 processor
- At least 2M or more of conventional RAM memory
- At least 5M disk space for minimum installation
- EGA or VGA graphics card, or graphics cards with proprietary Windows drivers
- 1.2M or 1.44M floppy-disk drive

Software Requirements

- Windows version 3.0 running in standard or enhanced mode
- MS-DOS 3.1 or later

An Overview of Excel 4.0

Microsoft Excel 4.0 is a powerful spreadsheet application developed for people at all skill levels. Spreadsheet programs are used in financial and scientific analysis of numeric data. Spreadsheet programs perform numerical calculations, illustrate relationships in numerical data by displaying charts, and help to organize data. Excel is easy for beginners, yet Excel also provides powerful features suited for programmers and high-level users.

This chapter highlights the main components of Excel 4.0, including worksheet capabilities, formulas and functions, formatting, charting, databases, and on-line Help. As you read through this chapter, you can assess the topics that will be of the greatest value to you. The chapters that follow cover each specific topic in greater detail. This chapter is an overview of Excel; it is designed to give you a general understanding of what you will learn in detail later in the book.

Objectives

1. To Understand the Excel for Windows Environment
2. To Understand Excel Worksheets, Charts, and Databases
3. To Access Excel's On-line Help
4. To Use Lotus 1-2-3 Skills in Excel for Windows

1

Key Terms in This Chapter	
Graphical user interface	A computer environment that uses a mouse, windows, icons, and a consistent menu structure to make computing more intuitive
Icon	A small picture that represents an application program (such as Excel), an accessory, or a file
Pull-down menu	A title on the menu bar that displays a list of commands when activated by the keyboard or mouse
Dialog box	A box that appears on-screen in Windows applications and requests information and input
Cell address	Location of a cell based on the intersection of the column and row in a worksheet
Active cell	The cell that receives the data you enter
Command	An order from you that tells the computer to carry out an action
Clipboard	A temporary storage location for selected information that is cut or copied from a worksheet
Functions	Predefined formulas included in Excel that simplify input of various types of calculations
Formatting	The process of changing and enhancing the appearance of text or data in a worksheet
Database	A collection of records organized into categories; used to conveniently store and later retrieve large amounts of information in a worksheet

Objective 1: To Understand the Excel for Windows Environment

By simplifying computer applications, Windows has transformed the way people use personal computers. Windows uses the operating system commonly referred to as *DOS*. Instead of interacting with the operating system through DOS commands, however, Windows uses a graphical user interface. This interface, called the *Windows environment,* employs icons (small pictures), a consistent pull-down menu structure, and dialog boxes. Windows programs can exchange data using a feature called the *Clipboard*. All of these features make a Windows program such as Excel 4.0 more intuitive so that users become productive with less effort.

Microsoft Excel 4.0 operates within the Windows environment. If you are comfortable working in a graphical environment, you will be at ease with the Excel basics. Many of the new features in Excel 4.0 have made spreadsheet computing even more graphical and easier to use.

Menus and Commands

The Excel window has a menu bar that displays nine menus. The File, Edit, Formula, Format, Data, Options, Macro, Window, and Help menus are listed across the menu bar. When selected, each menu on the menu bar displays a list of commands (see fig. 1.1). You can access a menu by using the mouse or the keyboard.

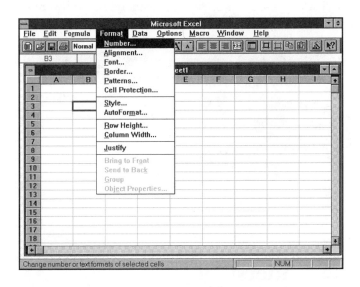

Fig. 1.1
The Format menu.

To access a menu with the mouse, point to the menu name and click the left mouse button.

1

To access a menu with the keyboard, press (Alt) to activate the menu bar. Then press the letter of the underlined character in the menu name. If you want to access the File menu, for example, press (Alt), and then press (F), the underlined character in the File menu name.

When you select a menu, a list of commands drops down. You then can choose a command from this drop-down list. To choose a command, you can use the mouse to point to the command and click the left mouse button, or you can press the underlined character in the command name on the keyboard. If you want to choose the Formula Paste Function command with the keyboard, for example, press (Alt) to activate the menu bar, press (R) to access the Formula menu, and then press (T), the underlined character in the Paste Function command.

If a command appears dimmed or grayed on a pull-down menu, the command is not accessible. If an active worksheet does not contain a link to another worksheet, for example, the Links command on the File menu appears dimmed or grayed.

Excel 4.0 enables you to access quickly some of the more commonly used Edit and Format commands in Excel. Edit commands—such as Cut, Copy, Paste, Clear, Insert, and Delete—and Format commands—such as Number, Alignment, Font, Border, and Patterns—appear on a shortcut menu when you press the right mouse button (see fig. 1.2).

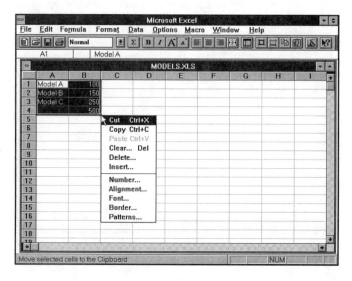

Fig. 1.2
The shortcut menu.

10

Dialog Boxes

When you access certain commands in Excel, a box appears in the center of your screen. This is a dialog box. Excel uses dialog boxes to request input from you or to confirm that you want to proceed with the settings defined in the dialog box (see fig. 1.3). The type of dialog box that appears depends on the command you choose. Some commands, such as the **Edit** Copy command, do not cause a dialog box to appear. Some dialog boxes contain several elements, but other dialog boxes request only a yes or no response from you before proceeding with the command. Chapter 3, "Excel Worksheet Basics," includes a section on dialog boxes. The section explains the different types of dialog boxes, the elements of a dialog box, and how to change settings in a dialog box.

Fig. 1.3
The dialog box
that appears
when you choose
the File New
command.

The Toolbar

The Excel 4.0 screen displays the Standard Toolbar across the top of the screen. The Toolbar is a group of tools, or icons, that represent commonly used commands. For example, if you want to make an entry bold, you simply can click the Bold tool on the Standard Toolbar to execute the command rather than choosing the Forma**t** Font command, selecting the **B**old option in the dialog box, and then choosing OK.

The Clipboard

The Clipboard is the part of your computer's memory that temporarily stores selected data, charts, or objects you cut or copy using Excel's Cut or Copy commands. After you cut or copy information to the Clipboard, you can place the information in another location on the same worksheet, on another worksheet, or in another Windows application. You can copy to the Clipboard information created in Excel, for example, and paste the information into Word for Windows or another Windows application.

1

Objective 2: To Understand Excel Worksheets, Charts, and Databases

You can use Excel's capabilities to calculate, store, and present data. This section describes the three main components of Excel: worksheets, charts, and databases.

What Is a Worksheet?

Sometimes referred to as an electronic spreadsheet, a *worksheet* is a grid with labeled columns and rows. Column headings are labeled with letters across the top of the worksheet; row headings are labeled with numbers down the left side of the worksheet. The intersection of a column and a row is called a *cell*. The *cell address* consists of the column letter and row number. B3, for example, is the cell address for the cell located at the intersection of column B and row 3.

A worksheet contains 256 columns and 16,384 rows, which means more than 4 million cells are available. You can record information in a cell in the form of text, numbers, formulas, or functions for calculating numbers. The *active cell* in a worksheet, defined by a bold border around the cell, is the cell that receives the data you enter. You can activate another cell in the worksheet by clicking the cell with the mouse or by using the arrow keys on the keyboard to move the cell pointer to the cell.

Typical uses of an electronic spreadsheet program such as Excel 4.0 include the calculation of budgets, student grades in a course, accounting problems, and expense accounts. Spreadsheet programs also are used for business plans, loan analysis, and scientific analysis. Because relationships within large volumes of numeric data are sometimes hard to interpret, these programs include the capability to create graphs, or charts, from worksheet data.

Formulas

The true power of using a worksheet for financial reports, income statements, budget forecasts, and other business applications comes from formulas. You can enter in a cell a formula that calculates numbers you have entered in other cells. A formula starts with an equal sign (=) and uses mathematical symbols (to indicate what type of operation the formula will perform) and cell addresses. The cell addresses identify the location of the data the formula will calculate. As you create the formula, it is displayed in an area of the worksheet called the *formula bar* (see fig. 1.4).

12

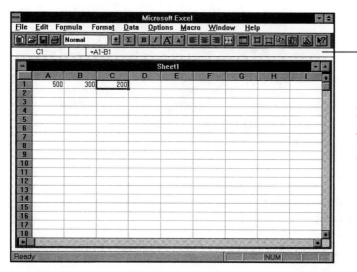

Formula bar

Fig. 1.4
A formula entered
in the formula
bar.

After you enter a formula in a cell, Excel performs the calculation for you. If
you change a number in a cell address that is used in a formula, Excel automatically recalculates the results of the change for you.

What-If Analysis

Entering a formula into a cell establishes a mathematical relationship among
the cells in the formula. A formula enables you to test results using different
numbers in the cells referenced in the formula. For example, if a formula
refers to a number in cell B10 and you type a new number in cell B10, the
cell containing the formula automatically recalculates the new result. Testing
results using formulas is sometimes referred to as *what-if analysis*. The
automatic recalculation of formulas is a useful feature in Excel 4.0 and other
electronic spreadsheets.

Worksheet Functions

You can use common mathematical operators to create simple formulas for
calculating data in a worksheet. The operators are + (to add), – (to subtract),
/ (to divide), and * (to multiply). In many cases, however, using one of Excel's
many built-in functions is much more efficient. A *function* is a prewritten
formula that takes a value, performs an operation, and returns a result in the
form of a value. The Formula Paste Function command displays a dialog box
that lists the categories of built-in functions (see fig. 1.5). The functions for the
selected category appear in the Paste Function list on the right.

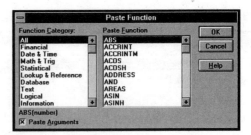

Fig. 1.5
The Paste Function dialog box.

A function simplifies the process of entering a formula. For example, instead of typing a formula, you can use Excel's PMT function for such operations as calculating the monthly mortgage payment for a 30-year loan with a fixed interest rate of 10 percent (see fig. 1.6).

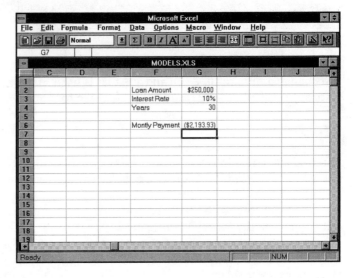

Fig. 1.6
Calculating a mortgage payment with the PMT function.

Functions enable you to easily perform various mathematical, statistical, logical, financial, and other business calculations. Chapter 6, "Using Functions," covers Excel functions in greater detail.

Formatting

Formatting one or more cells enables you to change the appearance of numbers or text in a worksheet. For example, numbers that represent money usually are formatted as currency (with a dollar sign and a decimal point).

1

If you are not sure what type of formats to apply, you can use Excel 4.0's AutoFormat command or tool. The AutoFormat feature enables you to apply a predefined format to a selected range of cells.

You can format numbers, using dollar signs, commas, or decimals; or you can format numbers so that negative numbers appear in parentheses. You also can format date and time numbers, using the Format Number command, and you can create custom number formats. The Number Format dialog box lists the categories of number types, including Currency, Percentage, Date, and Time (see fig. 1.7). Chapter 5, "Formatting a Worksheet," covers formatting in depth.

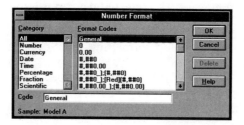

Fig. 1.7
The Number
Format dialog
box.

Formatting a worksheet also includes adjusting the column width and row height. See the section "Changing Column Width and Row Height" in Chapter 4, "Building a Worksheet," for these procedures.

What Is a Chart?

Charts, or graphs, are probably the most impressive way to represent data. If data is displayed in the form of a chart, the numbers are expressed in a visual manner that makes a strong impact on the viewer. Charts help people interpret worksheet data quickly.

To create a *chart* in Excel, you simply select the data you want to chart and press a single key, or you can use Excel's built-in ChartWizard. The charts you create are linked to the selected worksheet data. If you make a change in the data, the chart automatically is updated to reflect that change. After you create a chart, you are able to choose from 14 different chart types, including 8 two-dimensional and 6 three-dimensional types. Each of the 14 chart types has a selection of predefined chart formats (see fig. 1.8).

1

Fig. 1.8
A gallery of
predefined three-
dimensional
column chart
formats.

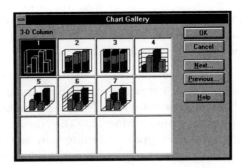

Double-click the chart format you want. The selected data appears instantly in
the selected chart format.

Chapter 8, "Charting Data," covers creating, formatting, and editing a chart,
and explains the ChartWizard.

What Is a Database?

You also can use an Excel worksheet to create a *database*. To create a database, you define field names or categories in the first row of the database, and
then you enter data in each row below in the form of a record (see fig. 1.9).
After you create a database, you can use Excel's Database commands to find
records that match certain criteria and to extract records from a database to
analyze or use in reports.

Fig. 1.9
Records in a
database.

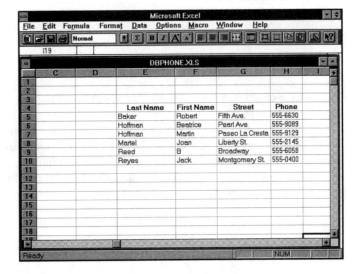

You can enter a database record in the worksheet cells or using the Data Form command. When you use the Data Form command, you enter data as though you were entering it on a form (see fig. 1.10).

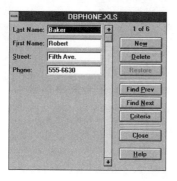

Fig. 1.10
Entering data in
the Data Form.

Chapter 9, "Managing Data," covers the multiple components of a database, including what a database is, how to build a database, and using Database commands.

Objective 3: To Access Excel's On-line Help

Excel contains comprehensive on-line assistance to help users at all levels with every aspect of the program. The Help menu is the last menu on the menu bar and also is represented as an icon on the Toolbar. On-line Help includes commands for Contents, Search, Product Support, Lotus 1-2-3 Help, Multiplan Help, and on-line tutorials to help new users get started with Excel.

If you have selected a command or if a dialog box is displayed on-screen, you can press F1 for a Help window. The window provides assistance on the selected command or dialog box. If you have not selected a command or if a dialog box is not on-screen, pressing F1 displays the Help Contents window (see fig. 1.11).

The Search button in the Help Contents window enables you to search for a specific Help topic, and shows you the selected Help topic and related topics. The History button enables you to return to previously accessed Help topics. Chapter 2, "Getting Started," explains Excel's on-line Help capabilities in greater detail.

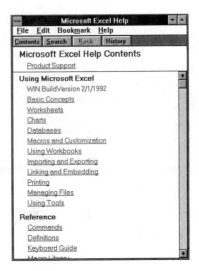

Fig. 1.11
The Help Con-
tents window.

Objective 4: To Use Lotus 1-2-3 Skills in Excel for Windows

If you are experienced with Lotus 1-2-3 spreadsheets, you will find that many of Excel's built-in features take advantage of your Lotus 1-2-3 skills. Some of the function keys in Excel, for example, are the same as those used in Lotus 1-2-3. Excel's Edit key is F2, Excel's Goto key is F5, and Excel's key for manual calculation is F9. If you want Excel to act even more like Lotus 1-2-3, you can modify Excel settings so that the movement keys in Excel work more like the movement keys in Lotus 1-2-3.

Excel's Lotus 1-2-3 Help feature enables you to use Lotus 1-2-3 procedures to execute Excel commands. You can set the Lotus 1-2-3 Help feature to display an instruction box that explains how to complete the Excel equivalent command, or you can set the feature to perform an on-screen demonstration of how to complete the equivalent command in Excel.

Summary

This chapter acquainted you with some of the features in Excel 4.0, and outlined the benefits of using a spreadsheet application for calculating, analyzing, charting, and presenting data. This chapter also covered the main components of working with Excel and some basic worksheet techniques.

Finally, this chapter included information about Windows, worksheets, formulas, functions, formatting, charting, database management, the Toolbar, and on-line Help. The specific topics are covered in greater depth in the chapters that follow.

Now that you are familiar with some of the features and capabilities of Excel 4.0, you are ready to learn how to use the program. Chapter 2 tells you how to start Windows and Excel. The chapter also presents mouse and keyboard techniques, and introduces you to the components of the Excel screen. You also will learn how to use on-line Help and tutorials.

Testing Your Knowledge

True/False Questions

1. The choices in the Excel menu bar, such as File, Edit, and Help, each have a list of commands associated with them.

2. A cell address in an Excel worksheet includes the row number followed by the letter of the column.

3. The * symbol is used to indicate multiplication in an Excel formula.

4. The / symbol is used to indicate division in an Excel formula.

5. An Excel function is used to change the appearance of numbers or text in a worksheet.

Multiple Choice Questions

1. Which of the following choices is a small picture that Windows uses to represent an application such as Excel?
    A. a cell
    B. an icon
    C. a clipboard
    D. a worksheet

2. A word (such as "Edit") in the menu bar of Excel indicates a
    A. function.
    B. cell address.
    C. dialog box.
    D. pull-down menu.

1

3. A predefined formula in Excel is called a
   A. function.
   B. file.
   C. database.
   D. macro.

4. A chart also is known as a(n)
   A. icon.
   B. menu.
   C. graph.
   D. format.

5. Which Excel command causes numbers to be displayed with dollar signs?
   A. Edit
   B. Help
   C. Format
   D. none of these answers

Fill-in-the-Blank Questions

1. You can use the _____ and the _____ to interact with Excel.
2. If Excel requires more information before it can execute a command, it displays a _____.
3. When you cut or copy selected information from a worksheet, it is placed in the _____.
4. "D5" is an example of a cell _____.
5. The cell that receives the data you enter is called the _____ cell.

Getting Started

2

If you are new to Windows, this chapter will help you understand the parts of the Excel window and some of the basic terminology. In addition to these topics, you will learn how to start Excel, how to use on-line Help and tutorials for assistance, and how to exit Excel.

If you are experienced with other Windows applications, you will be familiar with some of this introductory material. You may want to get acquainted with Excel's on-line Help features and then move on to Chapter 3.

Objectives

1. To Use the Keyboard and the Mouse in Excel
2. To Start Excel
3. To Understand the Excel Screen
4. To Use Excel's On-line Help and Tutorials
5. To Exit Excel

2

Key Terms in This Chapter	
Application window	The outer window identified by the application's name in the title bar
Document window	The window inside the application window that contains the document (your Excel worksheet)
Toolbar	An area of the screen that contains a series of icons you use to access commands and other features
Formula bar	The area at the top of the screen where you actually enter and edit data
Control menu	The drop-down menu located in the upper left corner of a window and represented by a hyphen inside a gray box, the Control menu icon; used for closing an application and for other commands
Context-sensitive Help	The on-line Help provided for a chosen command

Objective 1: To Use the Keyboard and the Mouse in Excel

Most of the interaction required in Windows and Windows applications is supported by the keyboard or the mouse. The mouse simplifies working in a graphical environment. Menus and commands are accessed by pointing and clicking with the mouse; objects and windows can be sized and moved by dragging with the mouse; and documents and programs can be loaded by double-clicking icons. Usually, you will want to use the mouse to interact with Excel. Sometimes, however, you may want to activate menus and commands from the keyboard.

Learning the Keyboard

To work from the keyboard, you need to be familiar with its structure. Most keyboards consist of four main parts: the alphanumeric keys, the direction keys, the numeric keypad, and the function keys (see fig. 2.1).

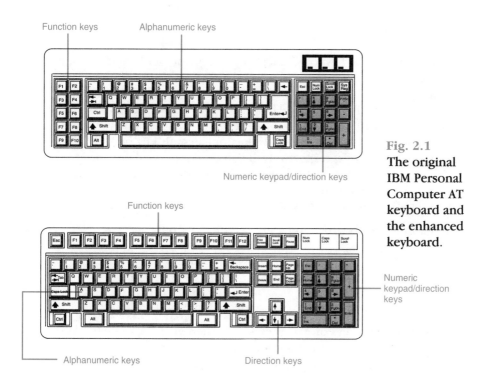

2

Fig. 2.1
The original
IBM Personal
Computer AT
keyboard and
the enhanced
keyboard.

Alphanumeric Keys

The alphanumeric keys make up the main portion of the keyboard. These keys are usually used for entering data or text. When you want to open a menu using the alphanumeric keys, you must first press (Alt) to activate the main menu bar. After you have activated the menu bar, press the underlined letter of the menu you want to access. The menu's list of commands drops down.

Numeric Keypad and Direction Keys

On some keyboards, the numeric keypad and direction keys are assigned to the same keys. When Num Lock is turned on, the numeric keypad is active, and you can use the keys like a calculator. When Num Lock is turned off, the direction keys are in control, and you can use them to move around a document or spreadsheet. Direction keys are identified on the keyboard by the up, down, left, and right arrows. Num Lock can be turned on at all times so that you can use the numeric keypad for data entry and calculations. The separate direction keys are not affected by Num Lock on enhanced keyboards.

2

Function Keys

The function keys on the keyboard are grouped together and are used for shortcuts for certain application commands. Some commands require only a function key; other commands require a function key in conjunction with the Shift, Alt, or Ctrl key. All standard keyboards have at least 10 function keys labeled F1 through F10. Enhanced keyboards have 12 function keys. For the commands assigned to the F11 and F12 function keys, Alt+F1 or Alt+F2 can be used for the commands, respectively, if you do not have an enhanced keyboard. The F11 function key, for example, is the shortcut key in Excel for creating a chart. On keyboards with only 10 function keys, the shortcut key combination for creating a chart is Alt+F1.

If you prefer to use keyboard commands, see the Appendix.

Exercise 1.1: Identifying Keys on the Keyboard

In this exercise, you identify some of the special keys used with Excel.

1. Find the function keys on your keyboard. Then, find the direction keys (the arrow keys) in the right corner of the keyboard.
2. Where is the Enter key and the Esc key on your keyboard?
3. Locate the numeric keypad. Is there a set of direction keys (arrow keys) that are separate from the numeric keypad?
4. Locate the Num Lock and Caps Lock keys on your keyboard. Does your keyboard have Num Lock and Caps Lock indicator lights in the upper right corner of the keyboard? If a light is on, what does it indicate?
5. Find the set of number keys at the top of the alphanumeric keys on your keyboard.

Using the Mouse

The mouse is an optional external device attached to your computer and is used for choosing menus and commands, editing and selecting text and objects, and moving and resizing windows. If you are new to the mouse, it may seem awkward at first. After you have experimented with the mouse, you probably will find that it is easier to use than the keyboard for moving around in a graphical environment. Your computer may be set up so that you can use the mouse only when Windows is running.

To operate the mouse, place your right hand on top of it. (If you are left handed, place your left hand on top of the mouse.) Position your index finger over the left mouse button, which is the only button you press to perform basic mouse techniques. The three techniques for operating the mouse are explained in table 2.1.

Table 2.1 Mouse Operating Techniques	
Technique	*Description*
Point and click	Position the mouse pointer on the item you want to select. Press the left mouse button once.
Click and drag	Press the left mouse button and hold it down as you gradually drag the mouse on a flat surface.
Double-click	Press the left mouse button twice in rapid succession.

As you gradually move the mouse on a flat surface, the mouse pointer moves on-screen. Depending on where you position the mouse pointer on-screen, the mouse pointer may change to another shape. The various mouse pointer shapes are detailed in table 2.2.

Table 2.2 Mouse Pointer Shapes	
Shape	*Description*
Arrow	Appears when the mouse pointer is positioned in a menu bar, scroll bar, or other area where an item can be selected
I-beam	Appears when the mouse pointer is positioned in the formula bar; used for changing the cursor location and selecting text
Cell pointer	Appears when the mouse pointer is positioned over the cells in the worksheet area; a cross-shaped marker used to select cells

continues

25

2

Table 2.2 Continued	
Shape	*Description*
Cross bar	Appears when the mouse pointer is positioned between row or column headings; used to change the row height or column width
Double-headed arrow	Appears when the mouse pointer is positioned on a window's border; used to resize the window
Split-screen arrow	Appears when the mouse pointer is positioned over the split bar directly above the vertical scroll arrow and to the left of the horizontal scroll arrow; used to split the worksheet area into divided sections
Magnifying glass	Appears in Print Preview mode; used to zoom in for a closer view of a section of the document to be printed
Help finger	Appears when the mouse pointer is positioned over a Help topic; used to move directly to the selected topic
Hourglass	Appears whenever Excel is executing a command; indicates that you must wait until the hourglass disappears to continue the next action
Autofill	Appears when positioned on the lower right corner of a cell or selected range. (The Cell Drag and Drop option must be turned on.) Used to fill adjacent cells with contents of the active cell.
Object sizing arrow	A double-headed arrow that appears when the mouse is positioned on the sizing handle of a selected object

After you start Windows (see the following section), you can practice using the mouse.

Objective 2: To Start Excel

Excel is a Windows application. Before you can start Excel, you must start the Windows program.

Starting Windows

Windows is a graphical computer environment that uses icons and pull-down menus to make computing easy and intuitive. Windows may already be running on your computer. If it is, you will see the Program Manager window on your computer screen. If Windows is not running, start Windows by typing **win** at the DOS prompt and press ⏎Enter). In some cases, you may need to be in the directory that contains the Windows files. To change to the Windows directory, enter **cd\windows** at the DOS prompt before you type **win**.

After Windows is loaded, the Windows Program Manager appears. The Program Manager is a window that contains several icons or windows called *program groups* (see fig. 2.2). A program group stores icons that are used to start an application. Each program group is labeled. One of the program groups may be labeled Microsoft Excel 4.0; it contains the Excel icon.

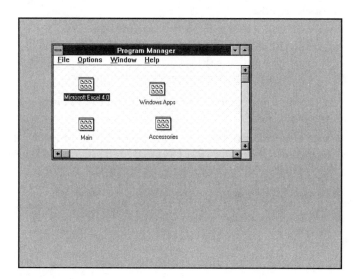

Fig. 2.2
Program groups
in the Program
Manager.

Now that Windows is running, you can practice some of the mouse skills you will use in Excel.

Exercise 2.1: Practicing with the Mouse

In this exercise, you practice moving the mouse and using the left and right mouse buttons. If you have not started Windows, do so now, and then follow these steps.

1. Locate your mouse and the left and right mouse buttons.
2. Can you see the mouse pointer on-screen? If so, what shape is it?
3. Move the mouse around on the desk to see how the mouse pointer moves on-screen.
4. Move the mouse around on the desk to position the mouse pointer in the lower right corner of the screen.
5. Move the mouse so that the mouse pointer points at each letter in the words Program Manager at the top of the screen. If the letter is an uppercase letter, click the left mouse button as you point at the letter.

   Note: Nothing will happen when you click these letters; this activity is just for practice.

6. Place the mouse pointer on the "M" in Program Manager and double-click the letter with the left mouse button. Practice keeping the mouse still (and the mouse pointer on-screen) while clicking the left mouse button twice in rapid succession.

   Tip: To hold the mouse pointer steady while you double-click, rest your thumb and little finger on the desk on either side of the mouse as you press down on the rear of the mouse with your palm. Place the mouse pointer, anchor the mouse with your hand, and then double-click.

7. Now click once with the right mouse button. Again, this activity is just for practice; nothing will happen.

Now that you can use the mouse, you will use it to start Excel. First, find the Excel icon. You may see a program group labeled Excel 4.0; if so, it contains the Excel icon. The Excel icon also may be stored in another program group labeled Windows Applications. If you do not see the Excel program group on-screen, double-click the Windows Applications program group. After you have found the program group containing the Excel 4.0 icon, you are ready to start Excel.

Starting Excel

Within Windows, you can use the mouse or the keyboard to start Excel. The sections that follow explain how to start Excel within Windows using the mouse because most users prefer to use the mouse. The Appendix contains many of the keyboard commands you can use with Excel 4.0.

Exercise 2.2: Starting Excel with the Mouse

In this exercise, you learn to start Excel with the mouse.

1. Make sure that Windows is running on your computer and that the Program Manager window is displayed on-screen.

2. Select the program group that contains the Excel 4.0 icon by placing the mouse pointer on the program group and double-clicking the program group with the left mouse button. Or click the program group once, and then click the Restore command on the menu that appears.

3. Point to the Excel 4.0 icon with the mouse pointer, and double-click the left mouse button. An hourglass appears on-screen, indicating that you must wait a few seconds for the program to load. When the program is loaded, the hourglass disappears, and you see the Excel screen (see fig. 2.3 in the following section).

Objective 3: To Understand the Excel Screen

When you start Excel, you will see the Excel screen. The parts of the Excel screen include the application window, document window (where you will build your worksheet), title bar, window sizing icons, menu bar, Toolbar, formula bar, scroll bar, worksheet area, and status line. Take a few minutes now to become familiar with the Excel screen; the descriptions in this chapter frequently will refer to the Excel screen's components (see fig. 2.3).

A brief description of each screen component is outlined in table 2.3. Some of the parts are described in more detail in the sections after the table.

2

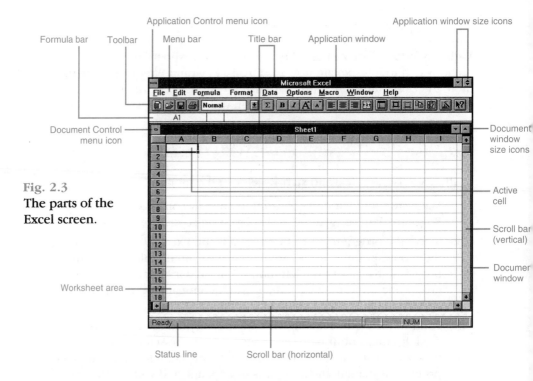

Fig. 2.3
The parts of the Excel screen.

Table 2.3	The Excel Screen
Component	*Description*
Application window	The outer window in which Excel runs
Document window	The inner window that contains the document
Application Control menu	Represented by a hyphen inside a gray box, the Control menu icon, in the upper left corner of the application window; used to move, size, and close the application window
Document Control menu	Represented by a hyphen inside a gray box, the Control menu icon, in the upper left corner of the document window; used to move, size, and close the document window

Component	Description
Title bar	Top portion of the window that lists the application or document name
Minimize button	Represented by the downward-pointing triangular icon; reduces the application window to a small picture on the desktop; reduces the document window to a small picture within the application window
Maximize button	Represented by the upward-pointing triangular icon; expands the application window to fit the entire screen; expands the document window to fill the application window
Restore button	Represented by the double triangular icon; restores the window to the middle size between minimized and maximized positions
Menu bar	Located directly below the title bar. Each menu contains a list of commands that drops down when the menu is activated.
Toolbar	Located between the menu bar and the formula bar; contains tools represented by icons for easy, graphical access to commands
Formula bar	Located above the document window; displays cell contents, and can be activated to edit cell contents
Scroll bars	Located along the right side and bottom of the document window; used to move the screen display horizontally or vertically; contain arrows and a box that moves along the bar as the arrows are activated

2

continues

31

2

Table 2.3 Continued	
Component	*Description*
Worksheet area	Enclosed by numbered row and lettered column headings. Worksheet cells are outlined by the intersection of a row and column.
Status line	Located at the bottom of the application window; displays a prompt line to tell you what a command will do or what to do next to complete the execution of the command

The Application Window

The *application window* is the outer window, with `Microsoft Excel` in the title bar. This window contains the menu bar, formula bar, Toolbar, and any open document windows. The application window does not contain scroll bars. To minimize, maximize, or restore the application window, use the window-size triangular icons in the upper right corner of the window. When the window is minimized, it appears as an icon on-screen (see fig. 2.4).

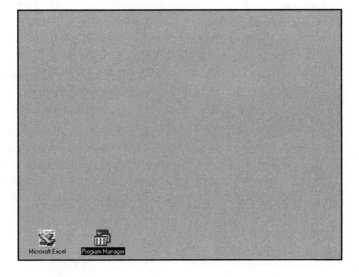

Fig. 2.4
The application window mini-mized as an icon.

You can restore the application to its previous position and size by double-clicking the icon.

The Document Window

The *document window* is the inner window that operates within the application window. The title bar of the document window contains the name of the document (your worksheet). If you have not yet saved a document to a file on your disk, Excel assigns a name to the document window. Excel assigns Sheet1, for example, to an unnamed worksheet, and Chart1 to an unnamed chart.

You can manipulate the document window in two ways. You can *maximize* the document window to fill the application window, or you can *restore* the document window to its previous size.

If a document window is maximized, the title of the document window appears in the title bar of the application window (see fig. 2.5).

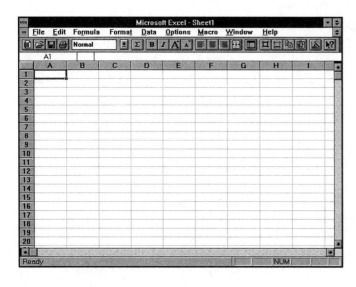

Fig. 2.5
The maximized document window.

If a document window is maximized and you want to restore the window to its previous size, click the double triangular icon in the upper right corner of the document window.

Exercise 3.1: Identifying Parts of the Application Window

2

In this exercise, you identify some important parts of the application window. If you have not started Excel, do so now, and then follow these steps.

1. Find the colored bar (usually colored blue) near the top of the screen. It should contain the words Microsoft Excel. This is the application window title bar.

2. Locate the two icons at the right end of the application window title bar. What is the gray box (with the hyphen in its center) at the left end of this title bar?

Exercise 3.2: Exploring the Mouse Pointer Shapes

In Windows and Excel, the shape of the mouse pointer changes to signal the operations you can perform with the mouse. In this exercise, you become familiar with some of these shapes.

1. Slowly move the mouse pointer around the various areas inside the application and document windows. Watch the shape of the pointer change.

2. Can you find an area in which the pointer becomes an I-beam pointer? What is this area of the screen called?

3. Is there an area of the screen in which the mouse pointer becomes cross-shaped? What is the area of the screen called?

4. Move the mouse pointer to the scroll bar at the bottom of the document window. Note the pointer's shape when it is inside the scroll bar.

5. Slowly move the mouse pointer out of the scroll bar to the bottom edge of the document window. Stop when the pointer becomes a double-headed arrow. Remember this position on the edge of the document window; you will use it in Exercise 3.4.

6. Check to see whether the mouse pointer becomes the double-headed arrow when it is on the top, left, and right edges of the document window.

2

The Control Menus

The application window and the document window contain separate *Control menus*, each represented by a hyphen inside a gray box, the Control menu icon, in the upper left corner of the window. The hyphen in the application Control menu icon is larger than the hyphen in the document Control menu icon. The Control menus share some of the same commands, such as **R**estore, **M**ove, **S**ize, **M**aximize, and **C**lose. Each Control menu also contains commands that are unique to its respective window.

The Window Sizes

A window can assume one of three sizes: minimized, maximized, or restored. The maximized size enlarges the application window to fill the entire screen. A document window can be maximized to fill the application window. To maximize a window, click the upward-pointing triangular icon (the Maximize button) in the upper right corner of the window. Or activate the window's Control menu, and choose the Maximize command. When a window is maximized, the maximize triangle is replaced by a double triangular icon (the Restore button) that restores the window. The restored size is the middle position between minimized and maximized. When a window is in the restored size, it has a border around the window; the border enables you to resize the window. When a window is in the restored size, you also can move the window.

To minimize the application window, click the downward-pointing triangular icon (the Minimize button) in the upper right corner of the application window. When an application window is minimized, it reduces to an icon on the desktop. To minimize the document window, click the downward-pointing triangular icon in the upper right corner of the document window.

When an application is minimized, it is still running, even though you cannot see the application on-screen. You can display the minimized window in its previous size by double-clicking the minimized icon on the desktop. In some cases, when you are not able to see your desktop, you are not able to see the icon representing the minimized window. If you cannot see the minimized icon on your desktop, activate the minimized window by using the Windows Task List (see fig. 2.6). To display the Task List, press (Ctrl)+(Esc).

Select the application from the Task List, and choose the **S**witch To command; or double-click the application you want to activate. The Task List box disappears from the screen when you select a command.

2

Fig. 2.6
The Task List.

Exercise 3.3: Changing the Size of the Document Window

In this exercise, you use the Minimize button to minimize the document window, and then you return the document to its original size.

1. Locate the document window on your screen. Its title bar should contain the word Sheet1.

2. Place the mouse pointer on the Minimize button (the downward-pointing triangle) on the right of the document window title bar. Click the left mouse button.

3. The document window should be minimized and appear as an icon labeled Sheet1 in the lower left corner of your screen.

4. Double-click the Sheet1 icon with the left mouse button. This action should restore the document window to its original size.

5. Look at the rightmost button in the document window title bar. Does its shape indicate that the document window is in the restored position, or is the window in the maximized position?

6. If necessary, click the Restore buttons to place both the application window and the document window in the restored position.

The Move and Resize Features

If a window is in the restored position, the window has a border around its outer edge. You can resize the window by clicking and dragging the window border with the double-headed arrow (see fig. 2.7).

A window must be in the restored position before you can move it on the screen. To move a window with the mouse, click in the window's title bar, and drag the window to the desired location.

Fig. 2.7
Resizing the
window.

2

————— Double-headed arrow

Exercise 3.4: Moving and Resizing the Window

In this exercise, you use the mouse to move the document window and to change its size.

1. To begin, make sure that both the document window and the application window are in the restored position.
2. Place the mouse pointer on the document window title bar. Click and hold down the left mouse button; drag the window to the left. Release the left mouse button.
3. Now click in the document window title bar, hold down the left mouse button, drag the window back to its original position, and release the mouse button.
4. Place the mouse pointer on the bottom edge of the document window. When it is in the proper position, the mouse pointer will change into a double-headed arrow.
5. Click and hold down the left mouse button, and drag the window edge up to the middle of the screen. Release the mouse button.
6. Use the same click-and-drag technique to pull the bottom edge of the window back to its original position.
7. Try the same resizing actions using the left and right edges of the document window.

The Toolbar

The *Toolbar* is a strip of icons displayed across the top part of the Excel application window. Excel's Standard Toolbar is designed to provide easy

2

access to common commands such as automatic summation, borders, print-ing, formatting, and styles. Table 2.4 describes what each tool does in the Standard Toolbar.

Table 2.4 The Toolbar	
Tool(s)	*Purpose*
	Opens a new worksheet; equivalent to choosing the **File New Worksheet** command
	Displays the dialog box for opening an existing file; equivalent to the **File Open** command
	Saves automatically the active named file; displays the File Save As dialog box if the file has not been named
	Automatically executes the **File Print** command, and begins printing the active document
	Lists predefined styles from a drop-down list, and enables you to apply a style to a selection
	Inserts SUM function and sums numbers directly above or directly to the left of the active cell
	Applies bold or italic formatting to the selection
	Increases font size; decreases font size
	Left-, center-, or right-aligns the selection
	Centers active cell contents across selected columns
	Applies predefined table formatting to the selected range; recognizes header rows and columns

38

2

Tool(s)	Purpose
	Applies a single-line border around the selected cell or range of cells
	Applies a border on the bottom of selected cells
	Copies selection to the Clipboard
	Pastes only formatting of cells copied to the Clipboard
	Activates the ChartWizard to create an embedded chart on the active worksheet
	Activates context-sensitive Help, placing a ? (question mark) next to the mouse pointer; selected command appears as a Help topic in a Help window

Exercise 3.5: Exploring the Toolbar

In this exercise, you use the context-sensitive Help tool to see the function of a tool on the Toolbar.

1. Click the Maximize button to place the application window in the maximized position.

2. Place the mouse pointer on the Help tool at the far right of the Toolbar, and click the left mouse button. The mouse pointer should now have a large black question mark attached to it.

3. Place the mouse pointer on the Bold tool (the tool with the **B** in the middle of the Toolbar). Click the left mouse button.

4. Read the information in the Help window that appears in the right half of the document window.

5. In the upper left corner of the Help window, double-click the Control menu icon.

6. You can use this same technique with the context-sensitive Help tool to learn the function of all the tools on the Toolbar.

2

The Formula Bar

The *formula bar* is located directly above the column headings in a worksheet (see fig. 2.8). The formula bar becomes active when you enter data into a cell. When the formula bar is active, a box with an X and a box with a check mark appear to the left of the area that displays the data you are entering in a cell.

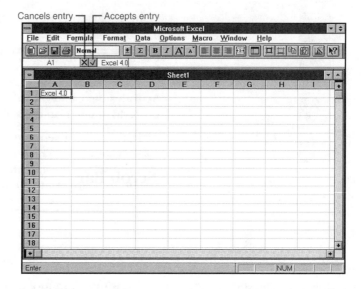

Fig. 2.8
The activated
formula bar.

To accept the entry, click the box containing the check mark or press ⏎Enter. If you do not want to accept the entry, click the box containing the X or press Esc.

To edit data after it has been entered into a cell, position the I-beam in the formula bar and click the left mouse button, or press F2. A blinking bar appears in the formula bar when the formula bar is activated, indicating the cursor's point of insertion. You can move the cursor in the formula bar with the arrow keys. Edit text using normal editing procedures. Press ←Backspace to delete characters to the left of the cursor. Press Del to delete characters to the right of the cursor. Press Ctrl+Del to delete to the end of the line.

In Chapter 3, you will use the formula bar to practice entering formulas.

The Scroll Bars

Because some worksheets are too large to be viewed completely on one screen, the document window contains horizontal and vertical scroll bars that

2

enable you to display other parts of the worksheets. The vertical scroll bar along the right edge of the document window represents the graphical equivalent of using the up- and down-arrow keys on the keyboard; the horizontal scroll bar along the bottom of the document window represents the graphical equivalent of using the left- and right-arrow keys.

Each scroll bar contains scroll arrows and a scroll box. As you click the up- or down- scroll arrows on the vertical scroll bar, the scroll box moves up or down the scroll bar. You can move to the top or bottom of the document by dragging the scroll box to the top or bottom of the vertical scroll bar, or you can place the mouse pointer in the scroll bar exactly where you want the scroll box, and then click. As you click the left- and right- scroll arrows on the horizontal scroll bar, the scroll box moves right or left in the scroll bar. You can move sideways in the document by dragging the scroll box right or left in the horizontal scroll bar, or you can place the mouse pointer in the scroll bar exactly where you want the scroll box, and then click.

Exercise 3.6: Using the Scroll Bar

In this exercise, you learn to use the scroll bars and scroll arrows.

1. Place the mouse pointer in the middle of the vertical scroll bar, which appears on the right edge of the document window. Click the left mouse button. What rows of the worksheet are displayed in the document window now?

2. Click the upward-pointing arrow at the top of the vertical scroll bar until the first row appears in the document window.

3. Place the mouse pointer in the middle of the horizontal scroll bar, which appears at the bottom of the document window. Click the left mouse button. What columns of the worksheet are displayed in the document window now?

4. Click the left-pointing arrow on the horizontal scroll bar until column A appears in the document window.

The Worksheet Area

The worksheet area covers most of the document window. This area is enclosed at the top by lettered column headings and on the left by numbered rows. The intersection of a column and a row defines a *cell*. A *cell address* is determined by the column and row intersection. Cell B6, for example, refers to the cell in column B, row 6.

Objective 4: To Use Excel's On-line Help and Tutorials

2

Excel contains two indispensable features that help you learn about the program: the on-line Help and tutorials. This section discusses both features.

Using On-line Help

Excel comes with a complete on-line Help system designed to assist users with commands and other Excel topics. This section provides you with an overview of how to use Excel's on-line Help system, search for a specific topic, back-track to previous Help topics, and print a Help topic.

The Help system is organized with a table of contents that divides primary topics into two categories: Using Microsoft Excel and Reference. Each category has topics listed below the category heading (see fig. 2.9). For assistance with learning how to create a chart in Excel, for example, you can find the Help topic Charts under the category Using Microsoft Excel. To see a list of worksheet functions, look for this topic under the Reference category. If you are familiar with Lotus 1-2-3 or Multiplan, see the Lotus 1-2-3 or Multiplan topics.

Fig. 2.9
The Help topics.

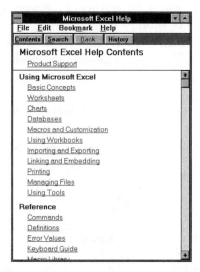

Exercise 4.1: Using Help Contents

In this exercise, you learn to access the Help index using the mouse. If you have not started Excel, do so now, and then follow these steps.

1. Open the Help menu, and choose the Contents command.

2. Use the scroll bar to scroll through the topics in the Help window. Place the mouse pointer on the underlined topic you want to select. The mouse pointer changes to a pointing finger. Click the left mouse button once.

3. To leave Help, double-click the Help window's Control menu icon in the upper left corner.

Searching for a Topic

The on-line Help system has a built-in list of Excel commands and key words. You can access a specific topic using the Search feature.

Exercise 4.2: Using the Help Search Command

In this exercise, you learn to search for a Help topic, using the Help Search command.

1. Open the Help menu, and choose the Search command. The Search dialog box appears (see fig. 2.10).

Fig. 2.10
The Search dialog box.

2. Use the scroll bar to scroll through the list of Help topics.

3. Select the topic you want in the list by pointing and clicking with the mouse. Then choose the Show Topics button.

2

4. Select the specific topic you want in the lower part of the dialog box. Then choose the Go To button. The Microsoft Excel Help window appears.

5. When you are ready, leave Help by double-clicking the Help window's Control menu icon.

If you prefer reading a sheet of paper rather than reading the screen, you can print a Help topic. First, select the Help topic you want. Then, open the File menu, and choose the **P**rint Topic command. The text in the active Help window begins printing. If you want to stop the Help topic from printing, choose the Cancel button.

Backtracking

When a Help window is displayed, you will notice four buttons below the menu bar of the Help window (see fig. 2.11). The four buttons include Contents, Search, **B**ack, and History.

Fig. 2.11
The Help window.

The Contents button displays the main Help window with the Help categories listed. The Search button enables you to search for Help on a specific topic or key word. The **B**ack button enables you to go back to previous Help screens. The History button lists all the Help topics you have accessed in a session and enables you to go back to a previous Help topic.

The **B**ack button displays the last Help topic screen viewed. The button continues backtracking in the order you viewed each topic until it reaches the Help Contents screen.

The History button is used to view previously selected Help topics. Each time a Help topic is selected, the title of the Help topic is listed in the History dialog box. To view a listing of all selected Help topics, choose the History button and select the Help topic you want to view again.

To use the mouse to choose a Help button, point to the button and click the left mouse button once.

Exercise 4.3: Using the Back Button in Help

In this exercise, you learn to use the **B**ack button in Help.

1. Open the **H**elp menu, and choose the **C**ontents command. The Help window appears. Notice that the **B**ack button in the Help window is gray. The gray button indicates that you are at the first screen, the starting point of this Help session.

2. In the list of topics, click `Worksheets`. The worksheet Help topics appear.

3. In the list of topics, click `Creating a new worksheet`. Help provides you with specific information about creating a worksheet.

4. Click the **B**ack button, which is dark now. After you click the button, you return to the screen where you selected `Creating a new worksheet`.

5. Click the **B**ack button again. Now you are back to the first screen you saw in Help. Notice that the **B**ack button is gray again. The gray button indicates that you have returned to the starting point of your Help session.

6. Click the Help window's Control menu icon to exit Help.

Context-Sensitive Help

Another way to access Help for a specific command is to use *context-sensitive Help*. To activate context-sensitive Help, choose the Help tool at the right end of the Standard Toolbar, or press ⟨⇧Shift⟩+⟨F1⟩. A question mark appears next to the mouse pointer. Select the command with which you want help. The Help window appears with the Help topic displayed for the command.

2

All Excel dialog boxes include a Help button (see fig. 2.12). If you don't know what to do when a dialog box is displayed, choose the Help button; a Help window displays the Help topic for the active dialog box.

Fig. 2.12
An Excel dialog
box.

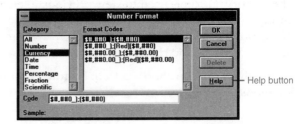

Help button

For more information about using Excel's on-line Help, activate a Help window by pressing F1 or choosing the Help tool. In the Help window, choose the How to Use Help command from the Help menu.

Working with On-line Tutorials

Excel 4.0 includes two commands under the Help menu for accessing inter-active tutorial lessons: Introducing Microsoft Excel and Learning Microsoft Excel.

The Introducing Microsoft Excel command includes three categories: The Basics, What's New, and For Lotus 1-2-3 Users (see fig. 2.13). The Basics provides an overview of the basic skills you need to get started using Excel. The What's New tutorial is intended for Excel users who only need to learn about the new features in Excel 4.0. The For Lotus 1-2-3 Users tutorial is designed to acquaint Lotus 1-2-3 users with Excel by comparing features in Excel with equivalent Lotus 1-2-3 features.

The Learning Microsoft Excel command includes six tutorial categories to help new users learn the skills necessary to take full advantage of Excel's extensive features (see fig. 2.14). The tutorial topics include Introduction, Worksheets, Charts, Databases, Macros, and Toolbars. At the beginning of each lesson, you see a display of the topics covered in the tutorial and the approximate amount of time required to complete the lesson. The tutorial guides you through the lesson with on-screen instructions and requests for input. You can exit the tutorial at any point in the lesson by using the Control menu.

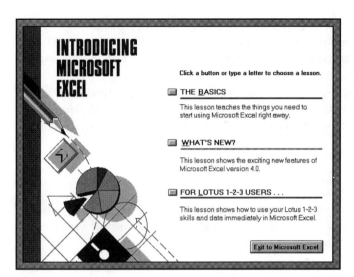

Fig. 2.13
The Introducing
Microsoft Excel
window.

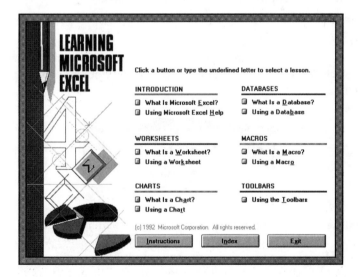

Fig. 2.14
The Learning
Microsoft Excel
window.

Exercise 4.4: Using Excel's On-line Tutorials

In this exercise, you learn to access Excel's on-line tutorial lessons.

1. Open the Help menu, and choose the Introducing Microsoft Excel
   command or the Learning Microsoft Excel command. Excel prompts
   you to save any open documents that have not been saved.

2

2. Select from the displayed lesson topics the tutorial you want to complete. The screen prompts you for input throughout the tutorial. Choose the Instructions button if you want to review instructions for using the tutorial.

3. When you are ready, choose Exit or press ⌊X⌋ to quit the tutorial. Choose the Main Menu button from the Control menu to return to the tutorial's main menu. You can select another tutorial.

Objective 5: To Exit Excel

At the beginning of this chapter, you learned how to start Excel. This section shows you how to exit, or quit, the Excel program. The following ways to exit Excel are available:

- Open the File menu, and choose Exit.
- Click the application Control menu icon, and choose Close.
- Double-click the application Control menu icon.
- Press ⌊Alt⌋+⌊F4⌋.

If you forget to save any open documents, Excel prompts you with a dialog box (see fig. 2.15). Select Yes to save any changes made to the document(s). Select No to lose the changes.

Fig. 2.15
The Save Changes
dialog box.

After the Excel program is closed, you return to the Program Manager in the Windows environment. The procedure to exit Windows works the same way as the procedure to exit Excel. Use any one of the four methods for exiting Windows. When you exit Windows, a dialog box asks you to confirm that you want to exit Windows. Choose OK or press ⌊↵Enter⌋ to exit Windows. Choose Cancel if you want to disregard the Exit command.

Exercise 5.1: Exiting Excel

In this exercise, you use the Control menu to leave Excel. If you have not started Excel, do so now, and then follow these steps.

1. Place the mouse pointer on the application Control menu (the gray box that contains a hyphen in the upper left corner of the Excel window).
2. Click the left mouse button.
3. Choose Close from the Control menu by placing the mouse pointer on the command and clicking the left mouse button.

Summary

In this chapter, you learned some of the fundamental techniques for starting and using Windows and Excel. Topics included keyboard features and function keys, mouse techniques, window components, and using Excel's on-line Help and tutorial features. You also learned how to exit Excel.

If you are comfortable with these Excel fundamentals, you are ready to move on to the next chapter. In Chapter 3, you will learn how to create a worksheet; enter data, formulas, and functions; select cells and ranges; access commands from the menu bar; and save, open, close, delete, and print a file.

Testing Your Knowledge

True/False Questions

1. If Windows is running on your computer, you will see the Program Manager window on your computer screen.
2. The cell pointer in Excel is a cross-shaped marker that appears over cells in the worksheet area and is used to select cells.
3. Menus and commands are accessed by pointing and clicking with the right mouse button.

4. The Open File tool on the Toolbar is equivalent to choosing the New Worksheet command from the File menu.

5. To exit from Excel, you double-click the application Control menu icon.

2

Multiple Choice Questions

1. The strip of icons displayed across the top of the Excel application window is called the
   A. formula bar.
   B. Toolbar.
   C. size bar.
   D. menu bar.

2. The downward-pointing triangular icon in the upper right corner of the application window is called the
   A. Autofill button.
   B. mouse pointer.
   C. Task List icon.
   D. Minimize button.

3. The gray box that contains a hyphen and appears in the upper left corner of the application window is called the
   A. application Control menu icon.
   B. status box.
   C. scroll bar.
   D. document Control menu icon.

4. To access the drop-down menu located in the upper left corner of the application window, you click the
   A. Toolbar.
   B. Status box.
   C. formula bar.
   D. none of these answers

5. In a worksheet, the intersection of a row and a column defines a(n)
   A. icon.
   B. bar.
   C. cell.
   D. none of these answers

Fill-in-the-Blank Questions

1. The _____ is an arrow that appears when the mouse is positioned in a menu bar, scroll bar, or other area where an item can be selected.

2. You start Excel by placing the mouse pointer on the Excel icon and _____.

3. To _____ means to press the left mouse button twice in rapid succession.

4. The _____ button is represented by the double triangular icon.

5. The _____ at the bottom of the screen displays what a selected command from one of the menus will do.

Review: Short Projects

1. Starting Windows

   If Windows is not running on your computer and the Program Manager is not displayed on-screen, follow the steps described in this chapter to start Windows and open the Program Manager.

2. Developing Mouse Skills

   When the Program Manager window is open, you will see a program group labeled Games. Open the program group, and double-click the Solitaire icon. Practice your mouse skills by playing one game. If you have questions about the game, use the Help menu. When you have finished, exit from Solitaire and return to the Program Manager.

3. Starting and Exiting Excel

   Follow the steps described in this chapter to start Excel. Then exit Excel and return to the Program Manager window.

Review: Long Projects

1. Introducing Microsoft Excel

   Start Excel, and use the mouse to open the Excel Help menu by clicking the word Help in the menu bar. Then choose the tutorial Introducing Microsoft Excel from the Help menu. Complete the first two lessons, The Basics and What's New? When you have finished, exit to Excel.

2. Learning More about Excel

Start Excel, and use the mouse to open the Excel Help menu by clicking the word Help in the menu bar. Then choose the tutorial Learning Microsoft Excel from the Help menu. Complete the two lessons in the Introduction, and then complete the two lessons in the Worksheets section. When you have finished, exit to Excel.

2

Excel Worksheet Basics

3

In Chapter 2, you learned the components of the Excel screen and some fundamental skills. Now you are ready to learn the basics of working in the Windows environment and of accomplishing a variety of common tasks in Excel.

In this chapter, you learn how to move around in a worksheet; create a worksheet; enter data, formulas, and functions; use worksheet commands; and print a worksheet. In addition to learning these skills, you will become familiar with commands that open and close a file and that name, save, and delete a file.

Objectives

1. To Move Around in the Worksheet
2. To Enter and Edit Text, Numbers, Formulas, and Functions
3. To Select Cells and Ranges
4. To Use Worksheet Commands
5. To Save, Open, Close, and Delete a File
6. To Print a Worksheet

Key Terms in This Chapter	
Cell pointer	A cross-shaped white marker that appears on-screen in the worksheet. You use the cell pointer to select the active cell with the mouse.
Cursor	A blinking bar in the formula bar, indicating the point of insertion
Edit mode	A mode in which the formula bar is activated and you can change the contents of active cells by using normal editing procedures
Range	A defined cell or group of cells on which Excel commands can act
File	When you save your Excel worksheet on a disk, the worksheet is saved in its own area. This area is called a *file* and must have a unique name. The name you use can contain up to eight characters. Excel adds the extension XLS to the file name. When you need to use a file that already is on a disk, you must open the file.
Extension	The last three characters of a file name, following the period. These characters identify the type of file or the file format.

Objective 1: To Move Around in the Worksheet

When you start Excel, a blank document appears in the document window on-screen. The document is titled Sheet1. Excel automatically assigns this name to the document until you save the document in a disk file and give the document a different name. The worksheet is the main document used in Excel for storing and manipulating data (see fig. 3.1).

A worksheet is made up of 256 columns and 16,384 rows. The columns are lettered across the top of the document window, beginning with A through Z and continuing with AA through AZ, BA through BZ, and so on, through column IV. The rows are numbered from 1 through 16,384 down the left side of the document window.

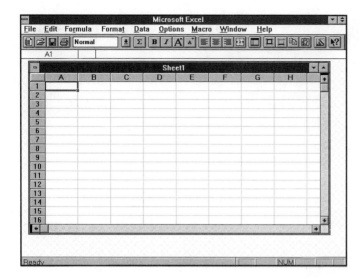

Fig. 3.1
The Excel
worksheet.

3

A *cell* is the intersection of a row and a column. The cell is the basic unit in the worksheet for storing data in the form of text, numbers, and formulas.

In a new worksheet, the cell at the intersection of column A and row 1 is outlined with a border that is darker than the other cells' borders. The darker border indicates that cell A1 is the *active cell*. If you start typing, the data appears in the active cell. To enter data into another cell, you must make the cell active by moving to that cell, using either the mouse or the keyboard. Moving to different locations in a worksheet is an important skill to master.

Moving the Active Cell

A mouse enables you to accomplish tasks easily in Excel. If you are using a mouse in a worksheet, you can make a cell active by placing the *cell pointer*, a white cross, on the cell and clicking the left mouse button once.

Using the keyboard, you can press the arrow keys, PgUp or PgDn, or key combinations to move to another cell and make that cell active. The keys you use to move to new locations are listed in table 3.1.

3

Table 3.1 Moving Among Cells with the Keyboard	
Key(s)	*Description*
⬅, ➡, ⬆, ⬇	Moves one cell to the left, right, up, or down, respectively. The new cell becomes the active cell.
Home	Moves to column A of the active row
Ctrl + Home	Moves to cell A1, the Home cell. The Home cell becomes the active cell.
PgUp	Moves up one screen
PgDn	Moves down one screen

You also can use F5 to move to a specific cell. When you press F5, the Goto dialog box appears on-screen (see fig. 3.2).

When the Goto dialog box appears, type in the **Reference** text box the address of the cell you want to make active, and then press ↵Enter. If, for example, you want to move to the cell in column D, row 5, type **D5** and then press ↵Enter or choose the OK button. Cell D5 becomes the active cell.

Fig. 3.2
The Goto
dialog box.

Exercise 1.1: Moving the Active Cell Using the Mouse

In this exercise, you make cell E10 the active cell. If you have not started Excel, do so now, and then follow these steps:

1. Place the cell pointer on cell E10.
2. Click the left mouse button. The dark border that indicates the active cell now appears around cell E10.

Exercise 1.2: Moving the Active Cell Using the Keyboard

Cell E10 currently is the active cell. To make cell C7 the active cell, follow these steps:

1. Press ← twice.
2. Press ↑ three times.

To go directly to cell H16, follow these steps:

1. Press F5.
2. When the Goto dialog box appears, type **H16**, and press ↵Enter. The active cell should be H16.
3. To return to the upper left corner of your worksheet, press Ctrl + Home.

Using the Scroll Bar

To view another section of the worksheet without changing the active cell, use the horizontal or vertical scroll bar. In Chapter 2, you learned the parts of a scroll bar and the way it works.

To view another worksheet section that is not visible, use the vertical and horizontal scroll bars to reposition the screen. If you see a cell you want to activate, place the cell pointer over the cell and click that cell to make it active.

Exercise 1.3: Using the Scroll Bar To Move Around in the Worksheet

In this exercise, you use the scroll bar to see another part of the worksheet on-screen.

1. Use the mouse to click the arrows in the horizontal and vertical scroll bars until you can see cell N30 on your screen.
2. Now click the scroll arrows until cell A1 appears again on your screen.

Note: Scrolling does not change the active cell.

Objective 2: To Enter and Edit Text, Numbers, Formulas, and Functions

After you activate the cell in which you want to enter data, you can type text, numbers, formulas, or functions in that cell. Entering data is how you build your worksheet. As you enter data, the data appears in the active cell and in the area above the worksheet called the *formula bar*. The formula bar displays the *cursor* (a blinking vertical bar), which represents the insertion point. Two small boxes also appear in the formula bar to the left of the insertion point (see fig. 3.3). The *cell address* of the active cell appears in the left end of the formula bar.

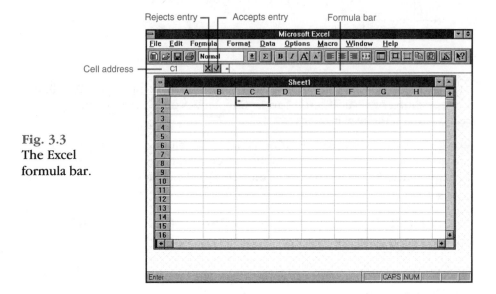

Fig. 3.3
The Excel
formula bar.

The left box displays an X; the right box displays a check mark. These boxes enable you to accept or reject the data you enter in the worksheet. The data you enter appears in the formula bar to the right of the two boxes. To accept your entry in the active cell, click the box containing the check mark or press ↵Enter. To reject your entry, click the box containing the X or press Esc.

To edit your entry, use ← and →, or move the mouse and use the on-screen I-beam to reposition the cursor in the formula bar. The vertical blinking bar

appears where the I-beam is positioned when you click the mouse. Then press
⌫Backspace or Del to delete characters to the left or right of the cursor,
respectively.

Entering Formulas

One of the most valuable features of a worksheet is its capability to calculate
results automatically by using a formula. Formulas also can refer to other
worksheet cells that contain numbers. Excel recognizes a formula in a cell if
the entry starts with an equal sign (=) or a plus sign (+).

To enter a formula, first type = (equal sign). Next, type the formula. If, for
example, three numbers have been entered into cells B1, B2, and B3, and you
want to display the total of those three numbers in cell B4, you type the
formula **=B1+B2+B3** in cell B4. Both the active cell and the formula bar
display the formula as you enter it.

Because the entry in cell B4 starts with an equal sign, Excel recognizes the
entry as a formula. After the formula is complete and you press ⏎Enter, cell
B4 displays the result of the formula. The formula bar continues to show the
formula whenever cell B4 is the active cell.

You can, unfortunately, make errors when entering cell addresses. If your
typing skills are less than adequate or you want to be more precise about
entering the exact cell address when you enter a formula, you may choose to
build a formula by selecting cells rather than by typing the cell addresses. You
can use the mouse or the keyboard to select cells for use in a formula.

Suppose that you want to build in cell D9 a formula that subtracts the total in
cell C9 from the total in cell B9. To build the formula with the mouse, follow
these steps:

1. Type an equal sign (=) in cell D9 to start the formula.
2. Click cell B9 to add the cell address to the formula in the formula bar.
3. Type a minus sign (–).
4. Click cell C9 to add the cell address to the formula.
5. Click the check box in the formula bar or press ⏎Enter to complete
   the formula entry. The complete formula is entered in cell D9, with
   the result displayed in that cell and the formula displayed in the
   formula bar (see fig. 3.4).

3

59

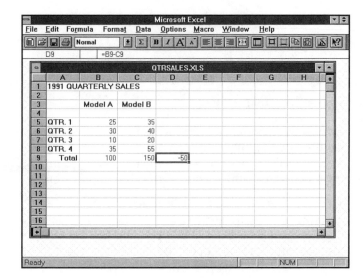

Fig. 3.4
A formula entered
in a worksheet.

Exercise 2.1: Entering Numbers in Cells and Adding Them

To enter numbers in the top three rows of column B and then add them, follow these steps:

1. Make cell B1 the active cell, and type 5.
2. Make cell B2 the active cell, and type 8.
3. Make cell B3 the active cell, and type 9.
4. Make cell B4 the active cell, and type the following formula:

   =B1+B2+B3

5. Press ⏎Enter.
6. Make cell B1 the active cell, type 200, and then press ⏎Enter. This entry replaces the old contents of cell B1. Notice that the result in cell B4 changes because cell B1 changed.

Using Mathematical Operators

When you build a worksheet, you often enter numbers into cells. Excel recognizes numbers as data that can be calculated. At some point, you probably will want to perform a calculation that uses numbers entered into cells. The following mathematical operators are used in basic calculations:

+	Addition
–	Subtraction
*	Multiplication
/	Division
%	Percentages
^	Exponentiation

Remember that errors often occur when mathematical operators do not appear in the *order of precedence*—the order in which calculations take place. The order of precedence for mathematical operations in a formula is as follows:

^	Exponentiation
*, /	Multiplication, division
+, –	Addition, subtraction

Exponentiation occurs before multiplication or division in a formula, and multiplication and division occur before addition or subtraction. If a formula includes mathematical operators that are at the same level in the order of precedence, the calculations are evaluated from left to right. If, for example, a formula includes addition and subtraction, and the addition operation appears in the formula first, Excel performs the addition before the subtraction.

You can use parentheses around mathematical operations that are part of a long formula. Operations enclosed in parentheses are evaluated first.

Exercise 2.2: Correcting Formulas

The purpose of this exercise is to show you how (and how not) to enter a formula. This exercise also illustrates the importance of the order of precedence. To find the average of the numbers you entered in Exercise 2.1, follow these steps:

1. Use the worksheet you created in Exercise 2.1, which has 200 in cell B1, 8 in cell B2, and 9 in cell B3.

2. Make cell B4 the active cell, type =B1+B2+B3/3, and then press ⏎Enter). This formula instructs Excel to find the average by adding the three numbers and dividing by 3.

But notice that cell B4 does not contain the average, because B3 is divided by 3 before the addition occurs.

3. To enter the formula correctly, type =(B1+B2+B3)/3, and then press ⏎Enter.

3 Using Built-In Functions

If you are working with only a few cells, building a formula by typing the formula and selecting cells may not seem too difficult. In many cases, however, your formula will involve several cells or groups of cells, and typing formulas and selecting cells may prove cumbersome and inaccurate. Excel's built-in functions enable you to easily create a formula that involves several cells or groups of cells.

A *function* is a predefined formula that consists of the equal sign (=), the function name, and the *argument* (cells Excel will use to perform the calculation). The SUM function, for example, adds the numbers in selected cells. The selected cells make up the argument portion of the function. The result of the function appears in the active cell. Fig. 3.5 shows a formula that uses the SUM function to total the entries in cells B1, B2, and B3.

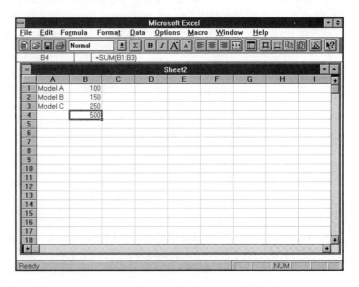

Fig. 3.5
A formula using a
SUM function.

To enter a function into the active cell, you can type = (equal sign), followed by the function name (**SUM**), followed by an opening parenthesis. Then you can enter the cell or range of cells you want the function to use, followed by a closing parenthesis.

Excel comes with a large number of built-in worksheet functions. Functions are covered in detail in Chapter 6, "Using Functions."

3

Exercise 2.3: Using the SUM Function

You can use the SUM function to add the entries in cells B1, B2, and B3 in the worksheet you started in Exercise 2.1. Follow these steps:

1. Make cell B4 the active cell.
2. Type =SUM(B1:B3), and press ⏎Enter.

Editing Data

To replace a cell's contents with other data, you need not delete the data first; you can select the cell that contains the data you want to replace, and then enter the new data. New data entered into a cell replaces any data that currently exists in the cell.

To edit (rather than replace) a cell's contents, follow these steps:

1. Activate the formula bar to display the cursor.

   To activate the formula bar with the mouse, move the mouse pointer to the formula bar. The mouse pointer changes to an I-beam. Click the left mouse button. The cursor appears in the formula bar, indicating that you are in Edit mode.

   To activate the formula bar from the keyboard, press F2. The cursor appears in the formula bar, indicating that you are in Edit mode.
2. Select the cell that contains the data you want to edit, using the mouse pointer or the arrow keys.
3. Use normal editing procedures to change the selected cell's contents. If you need to move the cursor to another location in the formula bar, press ← or → to move the cursor one character at a time. To move the cursor in the formula bar with the mouse, move the I-beam pointer to the new position and click the left mouse button once.

3

To delete a character to the left of the cursor, press [Backspace]. To delete a character to the right of the cursor, press [Del]. To insert text, numbers, or other data, place the cursor where you want the information to appear, and then type the data. If you select a cell after entering Edit mode, Excel adds the selected cell's address to the formula bar. If you edit the cell incorrectly and want to cancel the changes you made, click the X box in the formula bar, or press [Esc]. The cell returns to the way it was before you made the changes.

Exercise 2.4: Editing the Contents of a Cell

In this exercise, you edit the function in cell B4 so that you double the contents of cell B4.

1. Make cell B4 the active cell, and press [F2].
2. Type *2 at the end of the SUM function in the formula bar, and then press [Enter]. This formula multiplies the result of adding B1, B2, and B3 by 2.

Objective 3: To Select Cells and Ranges

Sometimes you will need to perform actions on one cell or on a block of cells in your worksheet. Before you perform an action on one or more cells, you must select the cells. To select a single cell, make the cell active by using the movement keys.

You also can select several cells. A group of cells is called a *range*. You can use either the keyboard or the mouse to select a range or a group of multiple nonadjoining ranges.

To select a range with the mouse, follow these steps:

1. Place the cell pointer on a cell at a corner of the range you want to select, and hold down the left mouse button.
2. Drag the cell pointer over the range.
3. When you reach the end of the range, release the mouse button. The range is selected. The cells in the selected range are surrounded by a gray border. The first cell of the selection is the active cell and has a white background; the rest of the selected range is dark (see fig. 3.6).

To select multiple nonadjoining ranges with the mouse, follow these steps:

1. Place the cell pointer on a cell at a corner of the first range you want to select, and hold down the left mouse button.

2. Drag the cell pointer over the range.

3. Hold down Ctrl, and continue selecting other ranges.

Fig. 3.7 shows two nonadjoining ranges selected at the same time.

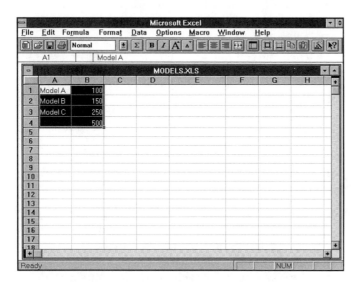

Fig. 3.6
A selected range.

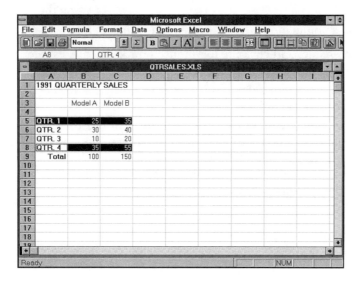

Fig. 3.7
Two selected
nonadjoining
ranges.

Exercise 3.1: Selecting a Range of Cells

In this exercise, you select the range of cells from cell B6 to cell E7.

1. Place the cell pointer on cell B6, and hold down the left mouse button.

2. Drag the cell pointer to cell E7, and release the mouse button. The thick cell border and darkened cells indicate that the range of cells in the block B6 to E7 are selected.

3. To deselect the range, click any cell outside the range (for example, cell F6).

Objective 4: To Use Worksheet Commands

After you build your worksheet by entering text, numbers, and formulas, you will want to save and print it. To instruct Excel to perform these and other operations, you use worksheet commands.

Every Windows application has a menu bar directly below the application title bar. Excel's menu bar has nine menus, starting with the **File** menu on the left and ending with the **Help** menu on the right. Each menu stores a group of commands. When you choose one of these commands, Excel carries out a specific task. To see a list of the commands for each menu, you must choose the menu.

To choose a menu and a command with the mouse, follow these steps:

1. Point to the menu name, and click the left mouse button once. A list of the commands drops down from the menu.

2. In this list, point to the command you want Excel to execute, and click the left mouse button once.

Certain Excel commands require you to perform a specific action before you choose the command. If, for example, you do not cut or copy something to the Clipboard, the **Paste** command in the Edit menu is not available and appears dimmed or grayed in the list of commands. If no object in the worksheet is selected, the commands that are relevant only to selected objects are dimmed and unavailable.

Using Dialog Boxes

In menus, the names of many Excel commands are followed by three periods (...). These periods, called *ellipses*, indicate that a dialog box appears on-screen if you choose the command. The dialog box requests additional information (such as command settings) or enables you to proceed with the command.

A dialog box can consist of different elements that display lists, enter text, select information, turn settings on or off, or cancel the command. The elements that appear in a dialog box depend on the type of command you chose. The Page Setup dialog box, shown in fig. 3.8, contains several elements.

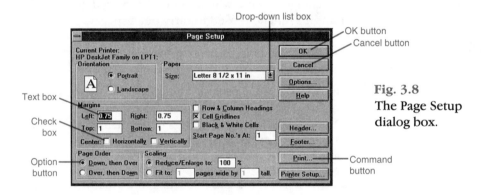

Fig. 3.8
The Page Setup dialog box.

Table 3.2 describes the elements shown in the dialog boxes.

Table 3.2 Dialog Box Elements	
Element	*Description*
Text box	A rectangular box used to display and enter information
Check box	A square box used to turn an option on or off. An X in a check box indicates that the option is turned on.
Option button	A circle that appears to the left of an option. If the option is selected, the circle is filled. You can choose only one option at a time in a group of options.

continues

67

3

Table 3.2 Continued	
Element	*Description*
Drop-down list	A list of options that drops down from a list box. To view the list, click the down arrow to the right of the box.
List box	A square area that displays the available choices. If all choices cannot be displayed in the square at one time, a vertical scroll bar appears on the right side of the box; use the scroll bar to view other choices in the list.
Command button	A rectangular icon, with a label describing the button's function, used to carry out a specific command. If ellipses (...) appears next to the label, another dialog box appears when you choose the button.
OK and Cancel buttons	Buttons that appear in most dialog boxes, enabling you to continue or discontinue the command. The OK button accepts the settings in the dialog box and proceeds with the command. The Cancel button cancels the command and closes the dialog box.

Making Selections within a Dialog Box

To activate a section of the dialog box with the mouse, point to the section with the mouse pointer, and then click the left mouse button once to choose an option button, turn a check box on or off, or choose a command button. To activate a text box, position the mouse pointer over the text box until the mouse pointer changes to an I-beam. Click the text box, and a cursor appears for data entry. To replace text in a text box, select the text by dragging the I-beam over the text, and then type the new text.

To choose an option in a drop-down list with the mouse, point to the down arrow at the right of the text box, and press the left mouse button once. The drop-down list appears when you click the down arrow (see fig. 3.9).

If the list requires scrolling, a vertical scroll bar appears to the right of the list. Point to the option you want, and click the left mouse button once. The drop-down list disappears after you make your selection.

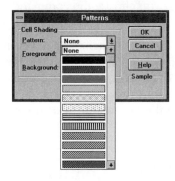

Fig. 3.9
A drop-down list.

3

Exercise 4.1: Using a Worksheet Command

In this exercise, you use the Format command to change the way numbers are displayed in cells B1, B2, and B3 of the worksheet you created in the earlier exercises in this chapter. To use the Format command, follow these steps:

1. Select the range of cells you want to format by placing the cell pointer on cell B1, holding down the left mouse button, dragging the cell pointer to cell B3, and then releasing the mouse button.

2. Place the mouse pointer on Format in the menu bar, and click the left mouse button. The Format menu drops down.

3. Choose Number by placing the mouse pointer on this option, and then clicking the left mouse button. The Number Format dialog box appears.

4. Place the mouse pointer on Number in the Category window, and then click the left mouse button.

5. Click 0.00 (the second choice) in the Format Codes window, and then choose OK.

The numbers in cells B1, B2, and B3 now should be displayed with two decimal places.

Using the Edit Undo Command

Excel has a built-in safety net that enables you to reverse many commands or actions. The Edit Undo command reverses the last command you chose or the

3

last action you performed. To undo a command or action, choose the Undo command from the **E**dit menu.

Caution: Excel retains only the last action or command, so you must choose the Undo command immediately after you choose the command or perform the action.

The Undo command is not available for all commands. If, for example, you choose the **F**ile **D**elete command and delete a file from a disk, the **E**dit menu contains the dimmed command Can't Undo. Although the Undo command can reverse many actions, you still must use certain commands with caution. To reverse the Undo command, open the **E**dit menu, and choose the **R**edo command.

Exercise 4.2: Using the Edit Undo Command

In this exercise, you undo an action.

1. Make cell B3 the active cell.
2. Type **123**, and press ⏎Enter. 123 appears in cell B3.
3. Click **E**dit in the menu bar, and then click **U**ndo Entry in the drop-down **E**dit menu. The contents of cell B3 should have reverted to what they were before you entered 123.

Objective 5: To Save, Open, Close, and Delete a File

Some of the most frequently used Excel worksheet commands involve files. When you are working with a worksheet, the data you enter or edit actually is stored in a temporary-memory area of your computer called *RAM* (random-access memory). If a power outage or computer failure occurs when you are working, the temporary memory is wiped out, taking with it the data you entered or edited. To avoid losing your work, you must save it frequently onto a disk. You usually also save your worksheet before you exit from Excel. When you save your worksheet on disk, you save it in a permanent-memory area called a *file*.

Saving and Naming a File

Your internal hard drive is the part of your computer that permanently stores information. A diskette also permanently stores data. To place a file in a permanent-storage area, you must issue a command to save the file, and then indicate on which disk drive (a:, b:, or c:) you want the file saved.

You must give the worksheet a file name if you are saving the file for the first time. The file name enables you (and Excel) to identify and find your file in the permanent-storage area on disk. When you save a worksheet you have just created, you must give it a name that is different from those of the other worksheets already on disk. Remember that each file name on your disk must be unique.

The File Save Command

To save a new file in Excel, open the **File** menu and choose the **Save** command, or click the Save tool in the Toolbar. The Save As dialog box appears on-screen when you are saving a file for the first time or when you choose the File Save **As** command (see fig. 3.10).

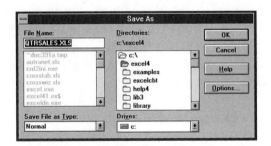

Fig. 3.10
The Save As
dialog box.

Type a name that will help you identify the worksheet in the future. You are limited to eight characters in a file name. These characters can include letters and numbers but cannot include spaces or periods. To use a space in a file name, use an underline (_) or hyphen (-) to separate characters. Excel adds a period and a three-letter extension to the file name. If you are saving a worksheet, the extension is XLS. A chart has the extension XLC.

If you want, you can save a file to another drive. Select the drive from the Drives drop-down list near the lower right corner of the Save As dialog box.

When you choose the **File Save** command to save changes in a file you already have saved and named, the File Save As dialog box does *not* appear. The **File Save** command overwrites the named file with the changes you made.

Exercise 5.1: Saving a Worksheet File

In this exercise, you save the worksheet you created in this chapter. You save this worksheet in a file named MYFILE. If you are saving files on your own disk, make sure that you have a formatted disk in the proper drive (a: or b:). Then follow these steps:

1. Open the **File** menu by clicking the menu name.

2. From the **File** drop-down menu, choose the **Save** command by clicking it. The Save As dialog box appears.

3. Type **MYFILE** in the File Name text box.

4. If you are saving on the hard drive (usually designated the c: drive), choose OK.

    If you are saving your file on a diskette, click the arrow to the right of the Drives drop-down list, near the lower right corner of the dialog box. Select your disk drive (a: or b:) by pointing to the proper letter with the mouse pointer and clicking the left mouse button. Then choose OK.

Now the worksheet is saved on disk under the name MYFILE. The document title bar should now display the name MYFILE.XLS.

Using the File Save As Command

Sometimes you may want to keep different versions of a worksheet in different files. In situations when you need to refer to a previous version of a document, you will want to have two copies of the document: one that contains the changes you make and one that does not have the changes. The **File Save As** command enables you to keep the original document and assign another file name to save the changed document. The Save As dialog box looks exactly like the dialog box that appears when you are saving an unnamed document for the first time (see fig. 3.11).

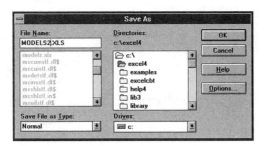

Fig. 3.11
The Save As
dialog box.

Exercise 5.2: Saving a File with the File Save As Command

In this exercise, you save your worksheet in a second file named MYFILE2.

1. Open the File menu by clicking the menu name.
2. From the File drop-down menu, choose the Save As command by clicking it. The Save As dialog box appears.
3. Type **MYFILE2** in the File Name text box.
4. If you are saving your file on a diskette, select the letter of the proper drive from the Drives drop-down list.
5. Choose OK to save the worksheet as MYFILE2.
6. Check to see that the document title bar now displays the name `MYFILE2.XLS`.

Now your worksheet has been saved twice—once as MYFILE and once as MYFILE2.

Opening and Closing a File

When you first start Excel, the program begins with a blank worksheet called Sheet1. When you want to work on a document that already exists, you first open the existing worksheet.

To open a file that already exists, open the File menu and choose the Open command, or click the Open tool in the Toolbar. The Open dialog box appears (see fig. 3.12).

73

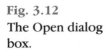

Fig. 3.12
The Open dialog
box.

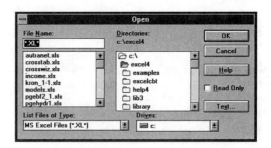

Using the File Name Text Box

The File **N**ame text box is selected when the Open dialog box is displayed.
You can open a file by typing the file name in the text box and choosing the
OK button or pressing ⏎Enter. The *.XL* in the File **N**ame text box indicates
that all files in the current directory ending with the extension XL plus any
other character will appear in the File Name list box. The asterisk (*) is a wild
card that is used to represent any other characters that may appear in the
requested order.

Using the File Name Box

The File **N**ame list box provides an alphabetical list of all Excel files in the
current directory. The current drive and directory are displayed above the
Directories list box. To select a file from the list with the mouse, place the
mouse pointer on the file name and then double-click the left mouse button,
or select the file name and choose the OK button. (Use the scroll bar, if
necessary, to view choices that are not visible in the list box.)

Using the Directories List Box

The **D**irectories list box displays all available directories and drives. This list
box enables you to locate a file in another directory or drive. To change to
another directory or drive with the mouse, place the mouse pointer on the
directory or drive name and then double-click the left mouse button, or select
the directory or drive name and then choose the OK button. (Use the scroll
bar, if necessary, to view choices that are not visible in the list box.)

Closing a File

When you finish working on a document, you will want to close the file. Open the **File** menu, and choose the **Close** command. If you did not save the file, Excel prompts you to save the changes before closing the document (see fig. 3.13).

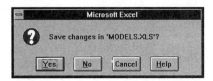

Fig. 3.13
The Excel prompt
for saving a file.

To close the document and save the changes, choose **Yes**. To close the document and ignore the changes, choose **No**. To close the dialog box and keep the document open, choose **Cancel**. If you saved all your changes before selecting the **File Close** command, you do not need to save again. The document window closes without prompting you to save changes.

Exercise 5.3: Closing a File

In this exercise, you close the active worksheet MYFILE2.

1. Open the **File** menu, and choose the **Close** command.

2. If the Save Changes dialog box appears on-screen, choose the **Yes** button if you want to save any changes you have made to the worksheet since you last saved it. Choose the **No** button if you do not want to save the worksheet before closing the worksheet. Either choice can be used in this exercise. Notice that the worksheet area disappears from the screen and that the menu choices are limited to **File** and **Help**.

Exercise 5.4: Opening a File

In this exercise, you open the disk file that contains the worksheet MYFILE. You need to remember on which disk drive (a:, b:, or c:) you saved the file when you performed Exercise 5.1. Follow these steps:

1. Open the **File** menu, and choose the **Open** command. The Open dialog box appears.

3

2. Check to see that the drive listed in the Drives drop-down list in the bottom right corner of the dialog box shows the correct drive. If not, click the arrow button to the right of the list, and then click the letter of the correct drive.

3. The names of the worksheet files on the disk appear in the File Name window. Place the mouse pointer on the file name MYFILE, and then double-click the left mouse button. The MYFILE worksheet should open in the document window, and the title bar should display MYFILE.XLS.

You now have the worksheet MYFILE available for use.

Deleting a File

Over time, you can accumulate many files. These files take up space on your hard drive. You can delete these files from within Excel by opening the **File** menu and choosing the **Delete** command. The Delete Document dialog box, which is similar to the Open dialog box, appears (see fig. 3.14). Select the file you want to delete from the File Name list box, and then choose OK; or double-click the file name.

Fig. 3.14
The Delete
Document
dialog box.

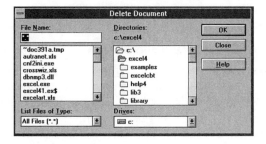

An alert box appears, asking you to confirm the deletion of the file. Choose **Yes** to delete the file; choose **No** to cancel the delete process.

Remember that you are deleting the file from a disk that is a permanent-storage location. If you do not have a backup copy of this file on a diskette, you cannot access the file again after you delete it. You cannot use the **Edit Undo** command to undo a file deletion. If a file has been deleted, the Cancel button will *not* cancel the file deletion. Choosing the Cancel button in the dialog box only closes the dialog box. Although file deletion is a convenient feature, you must use this command with care.

Exercise 5.5: Deleting a File

In this exercise, you delete MYFILE2 from your disk. Recall on which drive (a:, b:, c:) you saved this worksheet in Exercise 5.2. Then follow these steps.

1. Open the File menu, and choose the Delete command. The Delete Document dialog box appears.

2. Check to see whether the correct drive is listed in the Drives drop-down list. If not, click the arrow to the right of the list, and then click the letter of the correct drive.

3. Double-click the name MYFILE2, or click MYFILE2 once and then choose OK. An alert box appears, asking you to confirm the deletion.

4. Choose Yes in the alert box. You return to the Delete Document dialog box.

5. Choose the Close button in the Delete Document dialog box.

   MYFILE2 now is removed from the disk.

Objective 6: To Print a Worksheet

When you are building your worksheet or making changes in it, the worksheet must be in the computer's memory. When you have finished the worksheet, you can print it.

Note: To print, a worksheet must contain data.

If your worksheet has data in more columns than can print on one page, the column(s) at the right side of your worksheet will be printed on the second page of the printout.

Exercise 6.1: Printing a Worksheet

In this exercise, you print the worksheet MYFILE. (If MYFILE is not on your screen, use the File Open command to open MYFILE.) If your computer is not connected to a printer, you cannot complete this exercise. Follow these steps.

1. Make sure that your printer is on.

2. Click the Print tool in the Toolbar. The worksheet begins printing.

Summary

In this chapter, you learned many concepts that are crucial for using Excel, including moving around in a worksheet; entering and editing data, formulas, and functions; using worksheet commands and dialog boxes; selecting cells and ranges; and printing worksheets. Additionally, you learned procedures for opening, saving, naming, closing, and deleting files.

3

Summary Review Exercise: Entering, Saving, and Printing a Worksheet

In this exercise, you enter and save your first Excel worksheet. The worksheet is shown in fig. 3.15. Read all the steps before you begin. If you have questions, you may find it helpful to refer to Chapter 2.

Fig. 3.15
The FIRST.XLS
worksheet.

	A	B	C	D	E	F
1			ANNUAL SALES REPORT			
2						
3	REGION	QTR 1	QTR 2	QTR 3	QTR 4	TOTAL
4						
5	EAST	75000	71500	76000	65000	287500
6	SOUTH	10550	9345	8000	7500	35395
7	WEST	95400	97000	91550	93500	377450

1. Start Excel 4.0 by double-clicking the Excel icon with the left mouse button.

2. If you plan to save your worksheet on a diskette, make sure that a formatted diskette is in your diskette drive.

3. Make cell C1 the active cell by clicking it with the left mouse button. Type **ANNUAL SALES REPORT**. Then press ⏎Enter.

   Note: If you make a mistake typing in a cell or selecting from a menu, press Esc to start again.

4. Make cell A3 the active cell. Type **REGION** in cell A3, **QTR 1** in cell B3, **QTR 2** in cell C3, **QTR 3** in cell D3, **QTR 4** in cell E3, and **TOTAL** in cell F3. Press ⏎Enter after each entry.

5. Make cell A5 the active cell. Type **EAST** in cell A5, **SOUTH** in cell A6, and **WEST** in cell A7. Press ⏎Enter after each entry.

6. Make cell B5 the active cell. Type **75000** in cell B5, and press ⏎Enter. Fill in the remaining sales figures for quarters 1 through 4 by making the correct cell active, typing the number, and pressing ⏎Enter. Do not enter numbers in the TOTAL column; in the next steps, you will insert formulas in the column so that changes in quarterly sales are reflected in the new total.

7. Now you will enter the formulas that calculate total sales for each region. Make cell F5 the active cell, enter the formula **=B5+C5+D5+E5**, and press ⏎Enter.

8. Enter the formula **=B6+C6+D6+E6** in cell F6, and press ⏎Enter. Enter the formula **=B7+C7+D7+E7** in cell F7, and press ⏎Enter.

   Now your worksheet should look like the one in fig. 3.15.

9. Next, save your worksheet. You can do this by clicking the Save tool in the Toolbar. You also can save the worksheet by opening the File menu in the menu bar near the top of your screen, and choosing the Save command from the menu.

10. A dialog box should appear. Type **FIRST** as the name of your file.

    Note: If you are saving your worksheet on a diskette, double-click the letter of your diskette drive in the Drives drop-down list in the dialog box. If you are saving to the hard disk (the c: drive), do not click in the Drives drop-down list.

11. Click the OK button. Now your worksheet has been saved in a file named FIRST.XLS on the drive you selected. This name will appear in the document window title bar. You can exit from Excel now, and your worksheet will not be lost.

12. If your computer is attached to a printer, you can print your worksheet by clicking the Print tool in the Toolbar.

If you are comfortable with the information in this chapter, you are ready to start building a worksheet. In Chapter 4, you learn about working with ranges, changing column widths, copying cells, and inserting and deleting columns and rows.

Testing Your Knowledge

True/False Questions

1. The active cell in an Excel worksheet is outlined with a border that is darker than the other cells' borders.

2. To insert the formula-bar entry into the active cell, you can click the X box in the formula bar or press ⏎Enter.

3. If you turn off your computer, your Excel worksheet will be lost unless you have saved it in a disk file.

4. To select a range of the worksheet with the mouse, click a cell at a corner of the range, drag the cell pointer over the range, and then release the left mouse button.

5. To choose a command from a menu with the mouse, point to the command and click the left mouse button.

Multiple Choice Questions

1. The function key that enables you to go directly to a particular cell in the worksheet is

    A. F1.

    B. F2.

    C. F5.

    D. none of these answers

2. To view an area of your worksheet that is not on the screen, you can use the

    A. Minimize icon.

    B. scroll bar.

    C. =.

    D. Range command.

3. To change (edit) the contents of the active cell, you first press

    A. /.

    B. -.

    C. F2.

    D. *.

4. When you save your worksheet on a disk, the worksheet is saved in a

    A. file.

    B. active cell.

    C. range.

    D. extension.

5. Which of the following is a valid name to use when you store a worksheet on your disk?

    A. EXER 1

    B. EXER.1

    C. .XLS

    D. EXER1

3

Fill-in-the-Blank Questions

1. To save a file on the A drive of your computer, you select a: from the _____ drop-down list in the Save As dialog box.

2. To retrieve a worksheet you saved on a disk, you choose the _____ command from the File menu.

3. The formula you use to multiply the contents of cell D5 by the contents of cell E2 is _____.

4. The formula you use to add the contents of cell A3 to the contents of cell B3 and divide the sum by 4 is _____.

5. An Excel _____ is a predefined formula.

Review: Short Projects

1. Modifying an Existing Worksheet

   If you will use a diskette to save your worksheet, please make sure that a formatted diskette is inserted in the proper drive. Retrieve the FIRST.XLS worksheet from your disk.

   Enter TOTAL in cell A9. In cell B9, enter the formula to calculate total sales for QTR 1. Enter the formulas to calculate the respective total sales in cells C9 through F9.

   Change the contents of cell C5 to 100. Do cells F5, C9, and F9 change? Should any other cells change when you change the contents of C5?

   Save your revised worksheet in a file named SECOND.XLS. Exit from Excel, if you like.

2. Modifying Another Existing Worksheet

The worksheet SECOND.XLS must be open. In cell G3 enter **AVERAGE**, and in cell A11, enter **AVERAGE**. In cell B11, enter the formula to calculate the average sales for QTR 1. In cell G5, enter the formula to calculate the average sales for the EAST.

Fill in the appropriate cells in column G and in row 11 so that the proper averages are calculated. Do the averages change when the quarterly sales figures are changed?

Print the worksheet, and save the worksheet in a file named THIRD.XLS. You can exit from Excel, if you like.

3. Tracking Hours in a Worksheet

Set up your own worksheet in which you enter the hours you work (or study) each day of the week during a typical week. In your worksheet, also calculate total hours worked during the week and the average number of hours worked each day. Give the worksheet a name, and save it on your disk. If there is a printer attached to your computer, you can print your worksheet.

Review: Long Projects

1. Building a Calorie Worksheet

Assume that a friend is interested in losing weight. Your friend learned from a dietitian that 1800 calories per day will maintain your friend's weight at its current level. The dietitian also said that the friend will lose a pound a week if he or she consumes 3500 calories less than the 12,600 calories that would maintain his or her weight.

Your job is to construct a worksheet that will help keep track of your friend's diet. Your worksheet should look like the worksheet in fig. 3.16. Sample calorie counts are given, but your spreadsheet should be set up so that it will perform calculations when the daily calorie counts are changed. Name the worksheet C3LP1.

FIG 3.16
The calorie
worksheet.

	MON	TUES	WED	THURS	FRI	SAT	SUN
BKFAST	416	200	300	315	250	320	900
LUNCH	380	350	375	405	600	500	120
DINNER	800	700	600	590	1000	675	905
TOTAL	1596	1250	1275	1310	1850	1495	1925
MAINT =	1800	1800	1800	1800	1800	1800	1800
DIFFER =	204	550	525	490	-50	305	-125
TOTAL CALORIE DEFICIT =		1899					

2. Building a Payroll Worksheet

   Set up a worksheet that could be used to calculate a payroll. It should contain four columns: EMPLOYEE, HOURS, RATE, and PAY.

   No overtime is allowed. PAY is calculated by multiplying HOURS times RATE. Your worksheet should also compute the total amount of the payroll for this pay period.

3

Building a Worksheet

Chapter 3 covered a variety of topics, including moving around in a worksheet, entering data, saving files, using commands, and printing a worksheet. Now that you are familiar with some basic worksheet concepts, you are ready to learn more about setting up worksheets. Additional topics covered in this chapter include defining ranges; moving, copying, and clearing cell contents; inserting and deleting cells, columns, and rows; and changing column width and row height.

Objectives

1. To Use Ranges
2. To Move Cell Contents
3. To Copy Cell Contents
4. To Clear, Delete, and Insert Cells
5. To Insert and Delete Columns and Rows
6. To Change Column Width and Row Height

Key Terms in This Chapter	
Drag and Drop	A mouse procedure that enables you to move or copy data
Autofill	A procedure that enables you to copy data to selected adjacent cells
Clipboard	A temporary storage area that contains data you cut or copy
Marquee	Dashes that outline the area you cut or copy to the Clipboard
Fill commands	Commands that copy data in the active cell to surrounding cells
Relative cell reference	A cell address in a formula that adjusts to its new location when copied or moved
Absolute cell reference	A cell address in a formula that remains the same when copied or moved
Mixed cell reference	A cell address that contains a relative cell address and an absolute cell address
Best Fit	A command that adjusts the column width automatically to the widest cell in the column

Objective 1: To Use Ranges

A *range* is a group of cells. While building a worksheet, you can save time by applying a command to a group of cells rather than applying a command to individual cells. If, for example, you want to format the cell contents of several cells, select all the cells whose contents you want to format, and then apply the Format command. Any command or action you can apply to a cell you usually can apply to a range. Excel Format commands, such as **Number**, **Alignment**, **Font**, and **Patterns**, are commonly applied to a range (see fig. 4.1). You also can use ranges in functions.

A range can be any size. You can select a range using the mouse or keyboard. To select a range using the mouse, hold down the left mouse button and drag the cell pointer over the cells you want to select. To select a range using the keyboard, hold down ⇧Shift and use the arrow keys to select the cells. To select multiple nonadjoining ranges, select the first range as usual, and then select the remaining ranges by holding down (Ctrl) as you drag the cell pointer.

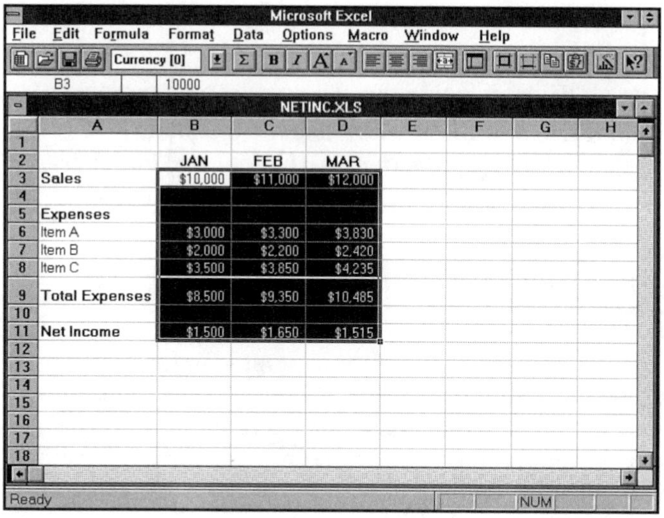

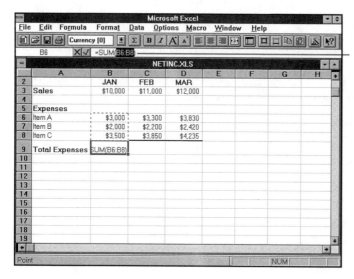

Fig. 4.1
A range formatted to display currency.

4

A function can refer to a range. If, for example, you are using the SUM function to add a group of numbers, select the range you want to sum. When a range is selected, the range address appears in parentheses in the formula bar. The cell address of the first cell in the range is followed by a colon and the cell address of the last cell in the range (see fig. 4.2). When referring to a range, B6:B8 means "cells B6 through cells B8."

Fig. 4.2
A selected range to use with the SUM function.

87

Exercise 1:1: Using a Range

Open the FIRST.XLS file you created in Chapter 3. You will use this worksheet in the exercises in this chapter. In this exercise, you select a range and change the size of the font in the range.

1. Select cells A3 through F3 by dragging the cell pointer over these cells.

2. Click the Increase font size tool in the middle of the Standard Toolbar. (This tool looks like a large letter A.) The font size in the cells increases.

4

Objective 2: To Move Cell Contents

When a worksheet is created, it is seldom perfect. At some point, a worksheet will require modifications. You might insert data in several cells, for example, and then decide that you want to place the data elsewhere in the worksheet. Rather than delete the data you entered and then reenter it in a new location, you can move the data to the new location. In Excel, you can move existing data to a new location in two ways. With the first method, Drag and Drop, you use the mouse pointer to move data. With the second method, Cut and Paste, you use the **Edit Cut** command to move selected data to the Windows Clipboard, and use the **Edit Paste** command to extract the data from the Clipboard and place the data in a new location. Remember, if you make a mistake as you are editing your worksheet, choose the **Edit Undo** command before you continue.

Moving Cell Contents Using Drag and Drop

Using the Drag and Drop method, you can move data from one location to another. To use this method, the Cell **Drag** and **Drop** option must be turned on. When this option is turned on, a thick, dark border with a square in the lower right corner appears around a selected cell or range (see fig. 4.3).

To turn on or off the Cell **Drag** and **Drop** option, follow these steps:

1. Open the Options menu, and choose the Workspace command. The Workspace Options dialog box appears.

2. If an X does not appear in the check box next to Cell Drag and Drop, select the check box so that it displays an X. The X indicates that the option is turned on.

   To turn off Cell Drag and Drop, select the check box again so that the X disappears.

3. Choose OK or press ⏎Enter.

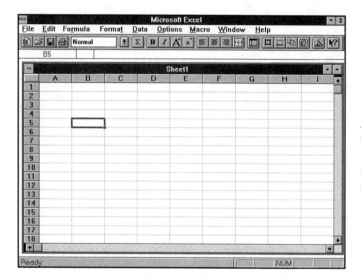

Fig. 4.3
A selected cell when the Cell Drag and Drop option is turned on.

To move data from one location to another using the Drag and Drop method, follow these steps:

1. Select the data you want to move.

2. Move the mouse pointer to a border of the selected data. The mouse pointer changes to an arrow.

3. Hold down the left mouse button, and drag to the new location. A border equal in size to the selection outlines the cell or area where the selection will appear (see fig. 4.4).

4. Release the mouse button to drop the selected data into the new location.

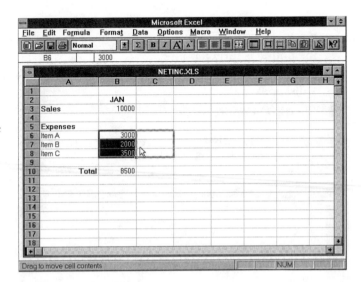

Fig. 4.4
The outline where the selection will appear.

Exercise 2.1: Moving with Drag and Drop

In this exercise, you use the Drag and Drop method to move the data in column F to column H in the FIRST.XLS worksheet.

1. Select rows 3 through 7 of column F.
2. Place the mouse pointer on the right edge of the highlighted data. The mouse pointer should change to an arrow.
3. Hold down the left mouse button, and drag to the new location (column H, rows 3 through 7).
4. Release the mouse button to drop the selected data into the new location.

Moving Cell Contents Using Cut and Paste

The Cut and Paste method uses the Clipboard to temporarily store information you want to move to another location. The **Edit Cut** command enables you to place selected data on the Clipboard. Using the **Edit Paste** command, you can paste information you placed on the Clipboard to another location. The Clipboard is explained in greater detail in the next section. To place information on the Clipboard, follow these steps:

1. Select the data you want to move.

2. Open the **Edit** menu, and choose the Cut command. A *marquee*, or small moving dashes ("the marching ants"), outlines the data you placed on the Clipboard (see fig. 4.5).

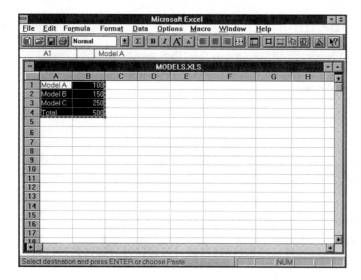

Fig. 4.5
A marquee
outlining data
that was placed
on the Clipboard.

3. Activate the first cell in which you want the data to appear. Then press ⏎Enter, or open the **Edit** menu and choose the **Paste** command. The selected data disappears from its original location and appears in the new location.

Select a single cell in which to paste data rather than a range. If you select more than one cell, the range you select must be equal to the range you placed on the Clipboard. If the ranges are different sizes, a dialog box appears. Choose OK or press ⏎Enter to clear the dialog box.

Exercise 2.2: Moving with Cut and Paste

In this exercise, you use the Cut and Paste method to move the data in rows 3 through 7 of Column H back to the old location in column F. Use your FIRST.XLS file.

1. Select rows 3 through 7 of column H.

2. Open the **Edit** menu, and choose the Cut command. A marquee appears around the data.

3. Activate cell F3, the first cell in which you want the data to appear. Then press ⏎Enter), or open the **E**dit menu and choose the **P**aste command. The selected data disappears from column H and appears in cells F3 through F7.

Understanding the Clipboard

Excel and all other Windows applications use the Clipboard for moving and copying data. The Clipboard actually is a section of computer memory that stores information temporarily so that you can move or copy information. Because the Clipboard is memory, information you place on the Clipboard is cleared when you turn off the computer.

You can place information on the Clipboard and relocate the information to other sections of the current document. The following reminders might help you understand how the Clipboard works:

- Your computer contains only one Clipboard for temporary storage.
- You can place only one item on the Clipboard at a time.
- You can place text or graphics on the Clipboard.
- The **E**dit **C**opy and **E**dit **C**ut commands place information on the Clipboard.
- The **E**dit **P**aste command extracts information from the Clipboard.

When you use the Clipboard, you can copy worksheet cells, formulas, and charts to locations within the same worksheet, to other worksheets, and to other applications. Using the Clipboard in this manner, you can build worksheets, ensure accuracy, and share information. Although you can access the Clipboard to see what is on it, you will seldom need to. For more information on how to access the Clipboard, refer to your Windows documentation or on-line Help in Excel.

To copy information to the Clipboard, select the information you want to copy, and then choose the **E**dit **C**opy command. A marquee appears around the copied information. The selected information has been copied to the Clipboard and can be pasted in another location.

After you cut or copy information to the Clipboard, you can place the information in another location on the same worksheet, on another worksheet, or in another application that supports the Clipboard. The **E**dit **P**aste command extracts information that is on the Clipboard to the selected location. Information you have copied to the Clipboard stays on the Clipboard until you use a Cut or Copy command again or until you turn off your computer.

Objective 3: To Copy Cell Contents

You can copy cell contents using one of three methods: Drag and Drop, Autofill, or Copy and Paste. With the Drag and Drop method, you use the mouse pointer to copy cell contents to nonadjacent cells within the same worksheet. With the Autofill method, you use the mouse pointer and fill handle to copy cell contents to adjacent cells. With the Copy and Paste method, you use the Clipboard to store contents you want to copy to another location within a worksheet, to other worksheets, and to other applications. Steps for each procedure are described in the following text.

Copying Cell Contents Using Drag and Drop

You use the Drag and Drop method to copy data from one location to another within the current worksheet. To copy data from one location to another using the Drag and Drop method, follow these steps:

1. Select the data you want to copy.

2. Position the mouse pointer on a border of the selected data. The mouse pointer changes to an arrow.

3. Hold down the left mouse button and press Ctrl. A plus sign appears next to the mouse pointer.

4. Drag to the new location where you want to place the copied data. A border equal in size to the selection outlines the cell or area where the selection will appear (see fig. 4.6).

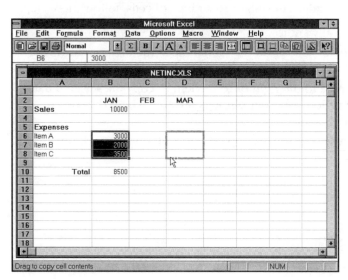

Fig. 4.6
The border where the copied data will appear.

5. Release the mouse button first, and then release the Ctrl key to drop the copied data into the outlined area.

Exercise 3.1: Copying with Drag and Drop

In this exercise, you copy the data in column A to column H in the FIRST.XLS worksheet, using the Drag and Drop method.

1. Select the data in cells A3 through A7.

2. Position the mouse pointer on the left border of the selected data. The mouse pointer should change to an arrow.

3. Hold down the left mouse button, and press Ctrl. A plus sign appears next to the mouse pointer.

4. Drag to Column H where you want to place the copied data.

5. Release first the mouse button, and then release the Ctrl key to drop the copied data into the outlined area.

Copying Cell Contents Using Autofill

Autofill is a method that enables you to copy cell contents to adjacent cells. You can copy cell contents to adjacent cells by using the Drag and Drop method or the Edit Fill commands.

With the Drag and Drop method, you use the *fill handle*, the black square in the lower right corner of a selected cell or range. To use Autofill to copy data from one location to an adjacent cell, or to a range of cells, follow these steps:

1. Select the data you want to copy to the adjacent cell(s).

2. Position the mouse pointer on the fill handle at the lower right corner of the selected border. The mouse pointer changes to a black cross.

3. Drag the fill handle to the right or to the left, to copy the selected data to the adjacent cell(s). A border outlines the area where the copied data will appear (see fig. 4.7).

4. Release the mouse button. The copied cell contents appear in the selected cell(s).

4

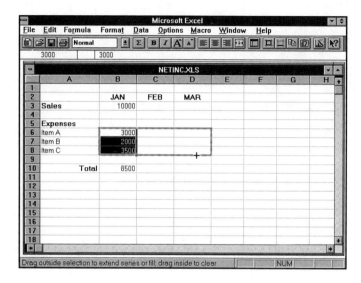

Fig. 4.7
The border where
the copied data
will appear.

4

Exercise 3.2: Copying with Autofill

In this exercise, you copy the data in cells H3 through H7 to column I in the FIRST.XLS worksheet, using Autofill.

1. Select the data in cells H3 through H7.
2. Position the mouse pointer on the fill handle at the lower right corner of the selected border. The mouse pointer changes to a black cross.
3. Drag the fill handle to the right to copy the selected data to the adjacent cells in column I.
4. Release the mouse button. The data should be copied in column I.

Copying Cell Contents Using Fill Commands

The Edit menu contains two commands for filling cell contents into adjacent cells: the Fill Right and the Fill Down commands. If you hold down ⟨⇧Shift⟩ before you open the Edit menu, these two commands change to Fill Left (**h**) and Fill Up (**w**), respectively. In figure 4.8, the selected cells are filled with the contents of the active cell.

95

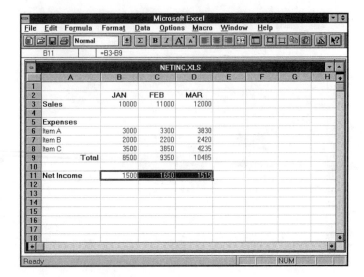

Fig. 4.8
Cell contents copied to the adjacent selected cells.

4

If the selected cells contain data, that data is cleared and replaced with the contents of the active cell. If you inadvertently replace existing data, open the **Edit** menu and choose the **U**ndo Fill command immediately after you perform the fill to reverse the action.

Filling a Range with a Numerical Series

In addition to copying a selected single row or column, Autofill also enables you to create a series of numbers based on data you already have entered in the worksheet. When you enter the numbers 5, 10, and 15 into consecutive cells within a single row or column, for example, Excel determines that this series contains increments of 5. Using Autofill, you can extend this series to 20, 25, and 30 and so on by selecting the range you want to fill and dragging the fill handle. To create a series from a selected range, follow these steps:

1. Select the data series within the row or column you want to extend.

2. Position the mouse pointer on the fill handle located in the lower right corner of the selected border. The mouse pointer changes to a black cross.

3. If the range you select is a column, drag the fill handle to the adjacent cells below. If the range you select is a row, drag the fill handle to the adjacent cells to the right of your selection. The selected cells in a column determine the series that will fit in the selected cells below (see fig. 4.9).

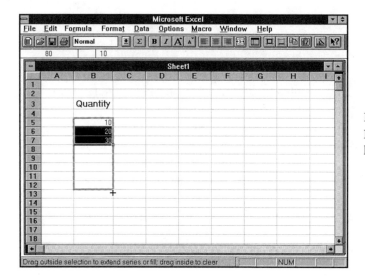

Fig. 4.9
Dragging the fill
handle.

4

4. Release the mouse button. The selected cells fill with numbers in the
   series (see fig. 4.10).

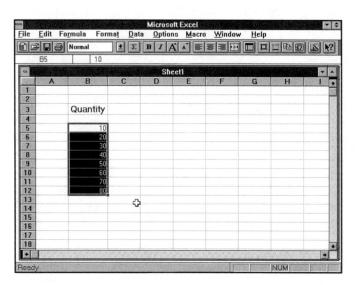

Fig. 4.10
The extended data
series.

Exercise 3.3: Filling a Range with a Data Series

In this exercise, you fill cells A12 through I12 with a data series in the FIRST.XLS worksheet.

1. Enter the number 1 in cell A12, and the number 3 in cell B12. Then select these two cells by dragging over them with the mouse.

2. Position the mouse pointer on the fill handle located in the lower right corner of cell B12. The mouse pointer changes to a black cross.

3. Because the range you are filling is a row, hold the left mouse button and drag the fill handle to the adjacent cells to the right of your selection until you reach cell I12.

4. Release the mouse button. Row 12 should fill with a data series.

Copying Cell Contents Using Copy and Paste

Copying cell contents is similar to moving cell contents. Rather than using the **Edit Cut** command, however, you use the **Edit Copy** command. After you paste the information, the copied information appears in the new location, and the original selection remains in its location. To copy information to the Clipboard, follow these steps:

1. Select the data you want to copy.

2. Open the **Edit** menu, and choose the **Copy** command. A marquee outlines the data copied to the Clipboard.

3. Activate the cell(s) in which you want the data to appear. Then press ⏎Enter, or open the **Edit** menu and choose the **Paste** command. A copy of the selected data appears in the new location, and the original data remains in the original location.

When you paste data into a cell, any existing data is replaced by the data you paste. If you inadvertently paste over a formula or other important cell contents, use the **Edit Undo Paste** command immediately after pasting to reverse the procedure. Excel restores the original data when the paste is undone.

When you copy information to the Clipboard, you can use the **Edit Paste** command to paste the information repeatedly. The **Edit Paste** command is available as long as the marquee outlines the copied data. If you paste the copied data by pressing ⏎Enter, the marquee that outlines the copied data disappears and the **Edit Paste** command appears dimmed, indicating that the command is not available. The marquee also disappears if you press Esc or if you begin to enter data in a cell.

Exercise 3.4: Copying Cells with Copy and Paste

In this exercise, you copy the number series in row 12 to row 14 in the FIRST.XLS worksheet, using Copy and Paste.

1. Select the data in cells A12 through I12.

2. Open the Edit menu, and choose the Copy command. A marquee outlines the data copied to the Clipboard.

3. Activate the cells in which you want the data to appear (cells A14 to I14). Then press ⏎Enter, or open the Edit menu and choose the Paste command. A copy of the selected data appears in the new location, and the original data remains in the original location.

4. If you used the Edit Paste command, you may want to remove the marquee from the worksheet by pressing Esc.

4

Copying Formulas to Multiple Cells

The capability to enter a formula and copy that formula down the rows in a column or across columns can save you considerable time in Excel. For example, if you need to total rows 5 through 8 of column C and display the result in cell C10, you would enter the formula =C5+C6+C7+C8 in cell C10. If you needed to calculate the totals for rows 5 through 8 of columns D, E, and F, you could copy the formula in cell C10 to cells D10, E10, and F10. Excel would adjust the formula when it is copied so that the formula would total the proper columns. For example, when the formula in cell C10 is copied to cell E10, the formula in cell E10 will be =E5+E6+E7+E8.

If you copy numbers or text in a worksheet, they are not changed when they are copied unless you are copying a series. Usually, formulas and functions *always* change when they are copied. Only if you use absolute cell references (these are discussed in "Absolute and Relative Cell References") will formulas and functions remain the same when they are copied. The formulas and functions change in a very logical and useful way that will become clear later when you look at some examples. First, you need to understand some general guidelines for copying cells in a worksheet.

If you copy the contents of a single cell, you can select multiple cells as a location for the copy. Then you can paste the copied data from the single cell into several cells. If you copy more than a single cell, the paste area you select must equal the area of the copied data. If you copy an area of five cells, for example, and you select an area of four cells in which to paste the data, a dialog box displays the message Copy and paste areas are different shapes. Choose OK, press ⏎Enter, or press Esc to clear the dialog box.

To avoid the problem of unequal copy and paste areas, select a single cell for pasting. When you select a single cell for pasting, the **Edit Paste** command pastes the data automatically into an area equal to the copied area. When you select a single cell for pasting, however, you might inadvertently paste over existing data. If you do paste over existing data, you can use the **Edit Undo Paste** command immediately after pasting to reverse the action.

In Excel, you can easily copy a formula from a single cell to multiple cells. In many worksheets, data is organized in a consistent format with formulas built to calculate the data. You might, for example, have several columns of data with a formula in the last row that adds the numbers in each column. In fig. 4.11, the formula bar displays a formula in cell B11 that subtracts the value in cell B9 from the value in cell B3.

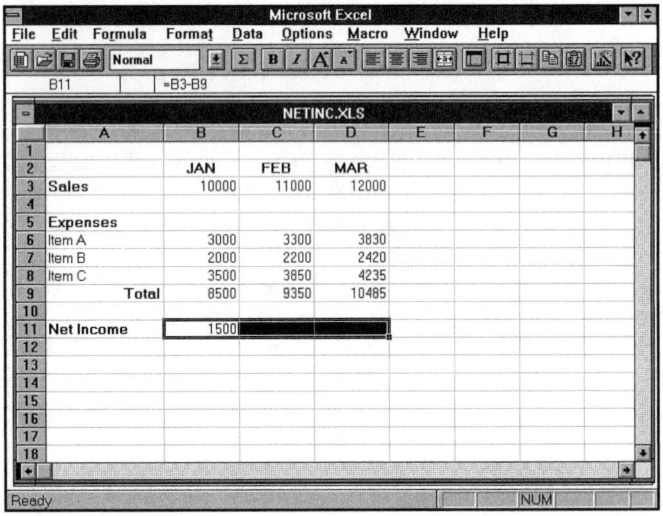

Fig. 4.11
The formula in cell B11.

While summing a range of numbers is not too difficult, some formulas are very long and complicated. Imagine if you had to enter a long, complex formula repeatedly. Rather than entering the formula manually each time, you could use the **Edit Copy** command to copy a formula to other cells and save a considerable amount of time. In the worksheet example, the user can copy the formula in cell B11 to the other cells, rather than type the formula in each cell. To copy a single cell and paste the formula in several cells, follow these steps:

1. Select the single cell that contains the formula you want to copy.
2. Open the Edit menu, and choose the Copy command.
3. Select the cells you want to contain the formula.
4. Open the Edit menu, and choose the Paste command.

Absolute and Relative Cell References

The procedures described earlier explain how to copy a formula to other cells. Remember that when you paste a formula or function, Excel takes the cell address in the copied formula and makes the cell address relative to the location of the pasted formula. If, for example, a formula in cell B11 displays =B3-B9 and this formula is copied and pasted to cells C11 through F11, the formula in cell C11 would display =C3-C9, cell D11 would display =D3-D9, and so on. The copied formula adjusts to the location in which it is pasted.

Cell addresses that adjust to a pasted location automatically are referred to as *relative cell references*. As you enter formulas, Excel assumes you want cell addresses to contain relative references. In some cases, however, you will not want relative cell references. For example, you might have a formula that refers to a single value in another cell, and regardless of where the formula is pasted, you want to refer to the value in that particular cell. If you want a cell address to remain the same wherever you paste the copied formula, change the cell address from a relative reference to an *absolute cell reference*.

An absolute cell reference is indicated by a dollar sign ($) in front of the column letter and a dollar sign ($) in front of the row number of the cell address. For example, $B$3 is an absolute cell reference. To make a cell reference absolute, enter a dollar sign ($) to the left of the column letter and a dollar sign ($) to the left of the row number of the cell address in the formula bar.

If the formula in cell B11 displays =$B$3-B9 and this formula is copied to other cells, the formula adjusts B9 relative to the location in which it is pasted. However, regardless of where the formula is pasted, the first part of the formula always refers to the value in cell B3. In fig. 4.12, the formula copied to cell C11 contains an absolute cell reference that always refers to the value in cell B3.

The types of cell references include relative, absolute, and two types of mixed cell references. Table 4.1 shows the types of cell references.

4

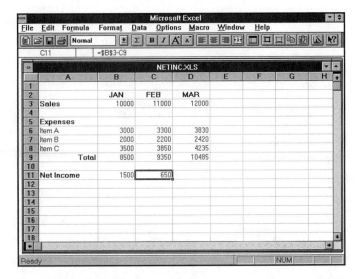

Fig. 4.12
A formula containing an absolute cell reference.

Table 4.1	Types of Cell References
Cell Reference	*Description*
A1	Relative cell reference. The formula adjusts to the relative location when copied or moved.
$A$1	Absolute cell reference. The formula refers to this cell always, regardless of where the formula is copied or moved.
A$1	Mixed cell reference. The formula always refers to row 1. The column adjusts to the relative location when copied or moved.
$A1	Mixed cell reference. The formula always refers to column A. The row adjusts to the relative location when copied or moved.

Mixed Cell References

In most cases, you will want a formula to contain either relative or absolute cell references. However, sometimes you will want the column reference of a cell address to remain the same (absolute reference) and the row reference to adjust to the relative position of the formula. A *mixed cell reference* enables you to have this flexibility. To mix cell references, place a dollar sign ($) in front of one cell component and not the other. If you want the column reference to remain the same regardless of where the formula is copied, for example, place a dollar sign ($) in front of the column letter. If you want the row number to adjust depending on the row in which the copied formula is pasted, do *not* place a dollar sign in front of the row number of the cell address. The formula =$B3–D9, for example, is a mixed cell reference. The column B reference is absolute; the row reference is relative.

4

Exercise 3.5: Copying Formulas with Relative Cell Addresses

In this exercise, you copy a formula with relative cell addresses in the FIRST.XLS worksheet.

1. Enter the formula =B5+B6+B7 in cell B9. Make sure that cell B9 is the active cell.
2. Open the Edit menu, and choose the Copy command. A marquee appears around cell B9.
3. Select cells C9, D9, and E9, the cells you want to contain the formula.
4. Open the Edit menu, and choose the Paste command. To turn off the marquee around cell B9, press Esc.

Exercise 3.6: Copying Formulas with Absolute Cell Addresses

In this exercise, you copy a formula with absolute cell addresses in the FIRST.XLS worksheet.

1. Enter the formula =$B$5+$B$6+$B$7 in cell B8.
2. Make sure that the formula calculates the correct total.
3. Use the same Copy and Paste technique you used in Exercise 3.4 to copy the formula in cell B8 to cells C10, D10, and E10.

   How are the formulas in C10, D10, and E10 different from the formula in cell B8? How are the formulas in C10, D10, and E10 different from the formulas in C9, D9, and E9?

103

Objective 4: To Clear, Delete, and Insert Cells

Excel provides two separate commands for deleting cell contents and deleting cells. The commands are **Edit Clear** and **Edit Delete**. Although the two commands sound as if they perform a similar function, they do not. You use the **Edit Clear** command to clear the contents of a cell, including formatting, formulas, and notes. When you clear a cell, the cell contents are removed, but the cell remains in the worksheet. You use the **Edit Delete** command to actually remove the cell from the worksheet. The **Edit Delete** command prompts you to move the surrounding cells to fill the space occupied by the deleted cell.

The two commands are often confused because (Del) on the keyboard is assigned to the **Edit Clear** command. When you press (Del), the Clear dialog box appears.

Clearing Cell Contents

The **Edit Clear** command deletes the contents of the selected cell(s) and leaves the cell(s) in the worksheet. When you choose the **Edit Clear** command, you use the Clear dialog box to select what you want to delete from the cell(s). The Clear dialog box provides the following four options:

All	Clears everything including formatting, formulas, and cell notes
Formats	Removes formatting only from the cell
Formulas	Clears formulas and maintains formatting and cell notes
Notes	Clears only notes attached to the cell

Exercise 4.1: Clearing a Cell or Range

To clear a cell or range, follow these steps:

1. Select the cell or range you want to clear. For example, select cells A12 through I12.

2. Open the Edit menu, and choose the Clear command. The Clear dialog box appears.

3. Select the option that represents what you want to clear from the cell. Select All by clicking the option button to the left of the option. Formulas is the default setting.

4. Choose OK or press ⏎Enter.

5. If you just removed something from your worksheet you didn't want to lose, choose Undo from the Edit menu.

Deleting Cells

When you delete cells from the worksheet using the Edit Delete command, Excel removes the cells and prompts you to move surrounding cells to fill the space of the deleted cells. The Delete dialog box appears when you select the Edit Delete command.

You can use the Delete dialog box to select how you want the surrounding cells to fill the space of the deleted cells. The Delete dialog box provides the following four options:

Shift Cells Left	Shifts surrounding cells to the left
Shift Cells Up	Shifts surrounding cells up
Entire Row	Shifts the entire row up
Entire Column	Shifts the entire column to the left

Exercise 4.2: Deleting a Cell or Range

To delete a cell or range, follow these steps:

1. Select the cell or range you want to delete. For example, select cells A14 through I14.

2. Open the Edit menu, and choose the Delete command. The Delete dialog box appears.

3. Select the option in the dialog box that represents the direction you want to move the surrounding cells. Select Shift Cells Up by clicking the option button to the left of the option.

4. Choose OK or press ⏎Enter. Based on the option selected, surrounding cells shift to fill the deleted space.

If you do not want the surrounding cells to fill the deleted cells, use the Edit Clear command.

Inserting Cells

Inserting cells in a worksheet is the reverse of deleting cells. The Edit Insert command prompts you to move surrounding cells to make space on the worksheet for the new cells, and then inserts the blank cells.

Exercise 4.3: Inserting a Cell or Range

To insert a cell or range, follow these steps:

1. Select the cell or range where you want blank cells to appear.
2. Open the Edit menu, and choose the Insert command. The Insert dialog box appears.
3. Make room for the additional cells by selecting the option in the dialog box that represents the direction you want to move the selected and surrounding cells.
4. Choose OK or press ⏎Enter. Based on the selected range, blank cells appear, and the selected cells and surrounding cells move according to the direction indicated in the Insert dialog box.
5. If you just inserted cells you don't want in the worksheet, choose Undo from the Edit menu.

Objective 5: To Insert and Delete Columns and Rows

You have learned to modify worksheets by inserting and deleting cells. Sometimes you will want to insert and delete column(s) and row(s). If you want to create additional space in the middle of a worksheet, you can insert a column or row that runs through the entire length or width of the worksheet. Conversely, if you have a column or row that is no longer necessary, you can delete the column or row rather than delete the cells.

Exercise 5.1: Inserting or Deleting a Column or Row

Follow these steps for inserting or deleting a column or row:

1. Select the entire column or row by clicking the column or row heading. For example, select row 10 by clicking the row heading, 10, at the left of your worksheet.
2. Open the Edit menu, and choose the Insert command to insert a blank column or row in the worksheet.
3. Open the Edit menu, and choose the Delete command to delete a column or row from the worksheet.

Edit Insert and Edit Delete are extremely useful commands; however, these commands can cause problems if you are not careful. Remember that when you are inserting or deleting a column or row, the entire length or width of the worksheet is affected by the change. You might have formulas or data in cells in another section of the worksheet that you cannot see; these cells might be affected by an insertion or deletion. If a formula refers to a cell that is deleted, the cell containing the formula displays the #REF! error value. To undo a deletion, open the Edit menu and choose the Undo Delete command immediately after making the deletion. This command reverses the action.

The Edit Insert command is a little more adaptable than the Edit Delete command. Formulas adjust to cell address changes when you insert a column or row; however, the command can disorganize areas of the worksheet. Always double-check your worksheet to verify worksheet results when using the Edit Insert or Edit Delete commands.

Objective 6: To Change Column Width and Row Height

One of the most frequently used worksheet commands is the command used to adjust the width of a column. When a cell contains data, the data often is cut off because the column is not wide enough to display the entire contents of the cell. If a cell cannot display an entire number or date, the cell fills with #########. After you widen the column sufficiently, the number or date appears in the cell. You can adjust the column width using the mouse or the keyboard.

4

To adjust the column width using the mouse, follow these steps:

1. Select multiple columns by dragging over the column headings. If you are adjusting the width of a single column, this step is not necessary.

2. Position the mouse pointer on the right border of the column heading. The mouse pointer changes to a double-headed horizontal arrow when positioned properly.

3. Drag the arrow to the right or left to increase or decrease the column width, respectively. A light gray outline indicates the column width. Release the mouse button when the column is at the width you want. The column width appears in the left end of the formula bar as you drag.

Exercise 6.1: Changing Column Width

In this exercise, you increase the width of column B in the FIRST.XLS worksheet.

1. Position the mouse pointer on the right border of the heading labeled B at the top of column B. The mouse pointer changes to a double-headed horizontal arrow when positioned properly.

2. Hold down the left mouse button, and drag the arrow to the right to increase the column width. A light gray outline indicates the column width. Release the mouse button when the column is in the middle of column D.

Best Fit Column Width

The Best Fit column width command enables you to adjust the column width to the widest cell in the column automatically. To access the Best Fit command using the mouse, position the mouse pointer on the right border of the column heading and double-click. The column adjusts to the widest cell in the column.

Row Height

Adjusting the height of a row works much the same as adjusting the width of a column. You can adjust the row height using the mouse or the keyboard.

To adjust the row height using the mouse, follow these steps:

1. Select multiple rows by dragging over the row heading numbers. If you are adjusting the height of a single row, this step is not necessary.

2. Position the mouse pointer on the bottom border of the row heading. The mouse pointer changes to a double-headed vertical arrow when positioned properly.

3. Drag the arrow down or up to increase or decrease the row height, respectively. A light gray outline indicates the row height. Release the mouse button when the row is at the height you want. The row adjusts to the new height.

Exercise 6.2: Adjusting Row Height

In this exercise, you increase the height of row 3 in the FIRST.XLS worksheet.

1. Place the mouse pointer on the border between the row 3 heading (at the left end of row 3) and the row 4 heading. The mouse pointer changes a double-headed vertical arrow when positioned properly.

2. Hold down the left mouse button, and drag the arrow down. A light gray outline indicates the column width. Release the mouse button when the row is in the middle of row 8.

Summary

This chapter covered many important worksheet features that are necessary for setting up ranges and moving or copying data. You also learned step-by-step procedures for inserting and deleting cells, rows, and columns. Additionally, you learned to adjust column width and row height. This chapter also introduced you to many fundamental concepts that can help you use Excel with greater efficiency.

Testing Your Knowledge

True/False Questions

1. A range in a worksheet can be used in a function or formula.

2. Before you can use the Drag and Drop method, you must turn on the option by using the Edit menu.

3. Relative cell references remain unchanged when a formula is copied to a new location.

4. In Excel, the width of a column can be increased but the height of a row cannot be changed.

5. If a cell's width is too narrow to display a number, Excel displays question marks in the cell.

Multiple Choice Questions

4

1. When placed on the Autofill fill handle, the mouse pointer becomes a
   A. double-headed arrow.
   B. white cross.
   C. black cross.
   D. dark rectangle.

2. Which character is used to make a cell address absolute in a formula?
   A. *
   B. $
   C. #
   D. none of these answers

3. To automatically adjust the column width to the widest cell contents in the column, place the mouse pointer on the right border of the column heading and
   A. click.
   B. double-click.
   C. press Ctrl.
   D. press ↵Enter.

4. When you paste data into a cell, any data already in the cell is _____ the data you paste.
   A. replaced by
   B. added to
   C. subtracted from
   D. none of these answers

5. The moving dashes around a cell that appear when Edit Copy is selected are called the

    A. Autofill.

    B. clipping.

    C. highlight.

    D. marquee.

Fill-in-the-Blank Questions

1. The _____ command from the _____ menu will undo an editing change in a worksheet.

2. A _____ is a group of cells in the worksheet.

3. The _____ is a temporary storage area containing data you can place in a worksheet using the Edit Paste command.

4. When using the Cut and Paste method to copy the contents of more than a single cell, the _____ area you select must equal the area of the copied data.

5. The Edit _____ command removes cells from the worksheet and prompts you to move the surrounding cells.

Review: Short Projects

1. Entering and Modifying a Worksheet

   Enter the worksheet shown in fig. 4.13, and save it on your disk as C4SP1.XLS.

	A	B	C	D	E	F
1						
2					QUIZ	
3	NAME	QUIZ 1	QUIZ 2	QUIZ 3	TOTAL	AVERAGE
4	ANDO	90	92	95		
5	BROWN	95	97	93		
6	CHANG	92	95	97		
7	JONES	90	91	100		
8	NGUYEN	97	96	95		
9	WATTS	98	100	97		

Fig. 4.13
The C4SP1.XLS worksheet.

Delete row 1. Then insert a blank row between the column headings and the data in the columns. Insert a new student, Mitchell, in a new row between Jones and Nguyen; assign grades to Mitchell. Change the

4

111

width of column A to accommodate the longest name now in column A. Use the Best Fit feature to adjust the width of columns B, C, and D. Make the row that contains the column headings twice as high as the other rows. Save the worksheet as C4PROJ1.XLS.

2. Adding to the Worksheet

Make sure that the C4PROJ1.XLS worksheet is open. Enter the formula to total ANDO's quiz scores in column E. Then copy the formula down the column so that the other students' totals are calculated. Verify that the formulas in Column E are correct. Give the name A_TOTAL to the cell that contains ANDO's total, and use this range name in a formula in column F that calculates her average. What would happen if you copied this formula down column F for the other students? Try it. Enter the formula to calculate BROWN's average, and copy the formula down column F. Check the results. Save this worksheet as C4PROJ2.XLS.

3. Completing the Worksheet

Make sure that the C4PROJ2.XLS worksheet is open. You decide that your students need another quiz because they aren't reading their textbook. Move the QUIZ TOTAL and AVERAGE columns to the right to make room for the QUIZ 4 column. Are the totals and averages still correct? Insert QUIZ 4 scores in column E; assign the scores. Correct the old TOTAL and AVERAGE formulas to reflect the addition of the new quiz. Save the completed worksheet as C4PROJ3.XLS, and then print it.

Review: Long Projects

1. The NSCC Company Quarterly Report

To help with a struggling new business, you are asked to set up an Excel worksheet to help the owner understand her cash flow. The completed worksheet is shown in fig. 4.14.

Fig. 4.14
The NSCC
Company
Quarterly
Report
worksheet.

	A	B	C	D	E	F
1			NSCC COMPANY QUARTERLY REPORT			
2						
3						
4		JAN	FEB	MARCH	APRIL	TOTAL
5						
6	EXPENSES					
7	PERSONNEL	90000	91070	92150	93400	366620
8	OFFICE SPACE	10000	10000	10000	10000	40000
9	TELEPHONE	2153	1417	2316	1728	7614
10	EQUIPMENT	5000	345	725	2972	9042
11	MISCELLANEOUS	1326	1508	1269	1301	5404
12						
13	TOTAL EXPENSES	108479	104340	106460	109401	428680
14						
15	SALES	97353	98934	102739	112953	411979
16						
17	BEFORE TAX PROFIT	-11126	-5406	-3721	3552	-16701

The expense figures for January through April are actual numbers, as are the sales figures for these months. However, cells F7 through F11, F13, F15, and F17 must all contain formulas (not just numbers) because the owner wants to continue to use the worksheet in the future. For the same reason, cells B13 through F13 and B17 through F17 should contain formulas. Remember: Profit = Sales – Expenses.

Save the worksheet as C4LP1.XLS (you will use it in later exercises), and then print it.

2. International Investment Analysis

   The worksheet you will complete for this project is used for investment analysis. The completed worksheet is shown in fig. 4.15. At this point, the worksheet is in a rough form. In later chapters, you will spruce it up and make some additions. No formulas or functions are in the worksheet yet. Simply type in the numbers, and save the worksheet for later use as C4LP2.XLS.

COMPANY	INDUSTRY	COUNTRY	(Mil.) SALES	(Mil.) NET INCOME	(Mil.) ASSETS	(Mil.) MARKET VALUE	PERCENT RETURN ON INVESTED CAPITAL
Solvey	Retail	Australia	11293	273	4262	3939	12.1
Kesko	Diversified	Brazil	6242	715	11684	9554	9.6
CNX	Automobile	Germany	12579	268	12059	2180	10.8
Dumez	Electronic	Italy	4283	66	2786	994	7.2
Nobunaga	Steel	Japan	11709	294	16036	8630	4.7
Nordlund	Optical	Norway	5476	291	5991	1438	9.7
Olnza	Machine	Spain	7602	1174	14114	14640	13.9
Lucus & Smith	Aerospace	U. K.	8272	160	8964	5415	7.3

Fig. 4.15
The worksheet you will use later.

Formatting a Worksheet

The appearance and layout of a worksheet can increase its usefulness and effectiveness. This chapter shows you how to improve the appearance of your worksheet by formatting. Whenever you *format* a part of a worksheet, you change the appearance of that element. You can format the text in a cell, for example, to appear bold or italic. You can format numbers to display as currency (with dollar signs) or as percentages (with percent signs).

This chapter covers formatting numbers, aligning cell contents (including centering text over multiple columns and making text appear vertical and horizontal), using automatic range formatting, justifying cell contents, changing fonts, and enhancing cells with borders and patterns. The chapter also covers the Standard Toolbar, and concludes with a topic vital to the professional appearance of your worksheet—spell checking.

Objectives

1. To Format Numbers
2. To Align Cell Contents
3. To Change Fonts
4. To Justify Paragraphs
5. To Format Cells
6. To Check Spelling

Key Terms in This Chapter	
Formatting	The process of changing the appearance of text, numbers, or cells in your worksheet
Predefined formats	Formats that already have been created and that come standardized with Excel
Toolbar	A group of icons that represent formatting commands and other commands for enhancing a worksheet
Style	A combination of formatting commands
Spell checking	A function that enables you to check worksheets, macro sheets, and charts for misspelled words, unusual capitalization, and repeated words

Objective 1: To Format Numbers

Because numbers are the most common items on a worksheet, Excel offers a variety of predefined formatting options you can apply to numbers. You may want a number to appear with two decimals in some places and with no decimals in other places on the same worksheet. You also may want to display negative numbers in red or in parentheses. Often you may want to display currency symbols or the percent sign without having to type the symbol every time you enter a number.

When you enter numbers, you do not need to be concerned with the way they look. After you have completed your entries, you can apply formatting to numbers and change the way they look on-screen or in print.

Excel offers you two different techniques for formatting numbers. You can use the Format menu, or you can use the Toolbar Style menu.

Applying Number Formats Using the Format Menu

To format numbers using the Format menu, follow these steps:

1. Select the cells that contain numbers you want to format.
2. Open the Format menu, and choose the Number command. The Number Format dialog box appears, displaying a list of predefined number formats (see fig. 5.1).

116

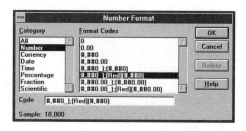

Fig. 5.1
The Number
Format dialog
box.

3. Select from the Category list the type of number format you want to apply. A list of predefined number formats for the category appears in the Format Codes list box.

4. Select the number format you want from the Format Codes list box. A sample of the selected format appears in the Sample area of the dialog box.

5. Choose OK or press ⏎Enter⏎. The selected number format is applied to the selected cells.

Exercise 1.1: Formatting Numbers Using the Format Menu

For the exercises in this chapter, open the FIRST.XLS worksheet you created in the first project at the end of Chapter 3. Then increase the width of columns B through F to at least 12; you will see the width displayed in the left end of the formula bar.

In this exercise, you format the number in cell B5 by using the Format menu.

1. Make cell B5 the active cell.

2. Open the Format menu, and choose the Number command. The Number Format dialog box appears, displaying a list of predefined number formats (see fig. 5.1).

3. Select the Currency category from the Category list. A list of predefined number formats for the Currency category appears in the Format Codes list box on the right.

4. Select the third format code ($#,##0.00) in the Format Codes list box. This code causes the number to be displayed with a dollar sign, a comma, and two decimal places.

5. Apply the number format by clicking OK or pressing ⏎Enter⏎.

117

Applying Number Formats Using the Style Menu

You can quickly apply commonly used number formats, such as Currency, Comma, and Percent, with the Style menu on the Toolbar. The Style menu on the Standard Toolbar includes predefined number formats that appear in a drop-down list (see fig. 5.2). Your choice of formats in this menu is more limited than in the Format menu.

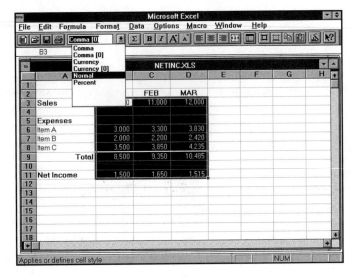

Fig. 5.2
The Style menu
on the Toolbar.

To apply a number format using the Style menu on the Toolbar, follow these steps:

1. Select the cells that contain the numbers you want to format.

2. Open the Style menu on the Toolbar by clicking the down arrow to the right of the Style menu.

3. Select from the drop-down list the number format you want to apply to the selected cells.

Your formatting choices are described in table 5.1.

Table 5.1 Number Formats on the Style Menu	
Format	*Description*
Comma	Adds commas to numbers that are 4-digits and higher. A number entered as 1000 is formatted as 1,000.

118

Format	Description
Comma (0)	Adds commas to numbers that are 4-digits and higher, and rounds decimals. A number entered as 1000.55 is formatted as 1,001.
Currency	Adds a dollar sign and two decimal places to the number. Adds a comma to numbers that are 4-digits and higher. A number entered as 1000 is formatted as $1,000.00.
Currency (0)	Adds a dollar sign to the number and rounds decimals. Adds a comma to numbers that are 4-digits and higher. A number entered as 1000.55 is formatted as $1,001.
Normal	Applies the style that defines normal or default character formatting. A number entered as 1000 is formatted as 1000.
Percent	Multiplies the number by 100 and adds a percent symbol to the number. A number entered as .15 is formatted as 15%.

5

Exercise 1.2: Formatting Numbers Using the Style Menu

In this exercise, you apply a number format to a range of cells, using the Style menu on the Toolbar. The notation B5:E7 means "the range of cells from B5 through E7."

1. Select the range B5:E7 by dragging over the cells with the cell pointer.

2. Open the Style menu on the Toolbar by clicking the down arrow to the right of the Style menu.

3. Select the Comma format from the drop-down list. The numbers in the selected range are displayed with a comma and two decimal places.

4. Return the numbers in the selected range to Excel's default format by choosing the Normal format from the Style menu.

Changing Date and Time Formats

If you enter 1-1-94 in a cell, Excel assumes that you are entering a date. The cell, therefore, displays the number in a date format. (The default date format is 1/1/94.) If you enter 9:45, Excel assumes that you are referring to a time, and displays a time format. To change to another date or time format, you can use the Format Number command. The procedure for changing a date or time format is the same as changing a number format. The date and time formats are separate categories of number formats. When you select the Date category in the Category list of the Number Format dialog box, the date format codes appear.

5

Objective 2: To Align Cell Contents

Sometimes you may want to change the way numbers or text are located within a cell. You can format numbers and text so that they appear left-aligned, right-aligned, or centered in a cell. You also can format text to wrap within a cell if the text is lengthy, or to appear centered across a range of columns, or to appear vertically. To *wrap* text within a cell means that a long string of text will appear on multiple lines within a cell. The height of the cell will continue to increase so that the cell can contain the lines of text as you type.

Caution: If numbers will be used in calculations, leave the numbers right-aligned. Numbers are right-aligned when you first enter them. Experienced Excel users leave the numbers that will be used in calculations right-aligned, and change only the text alignment in the worksheet. A common practice is to right-align the text headings on columns of numbers so that the headings appear directly over the numbers. Numbers that will not be used in calculations—such as phone numbers and ZIP codes—can be aligned just like text.

You can apply alignment formatting such as left, center, and right alignment, using the Standard Toolbar. The Format Alignment command enables you to wrap text, choose vertical alignment, and choose Orientation options for vertical text and sideways text. The steps for aligning data and text using both the Standard Toolbar and the Format Alignment command are outlined in the text that follows.

Aligning Data and Text

To align data or text using the Toolbar, follow these steps:

1. Select the cell or range in which you want to align data or text.

2. Click the Left-Align, Center, or Right-Align tool to apply alignment formatting to the selection. The three Alignment tools are located on the Standard Toolbar (see fig. 5.3).

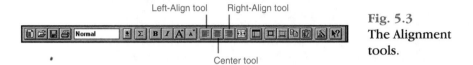

Left-Align tool Right-Align tool

Center tool

Fig. 5.3
The Alignment
tools.

To align data or text using the Format Alignment command, follow these steps:

1. Select the cell or range in which you want to align data or text.

2. Open the Format menu, and choose the Alignment command. The Alignment dialog box appears (fig. 5.4).

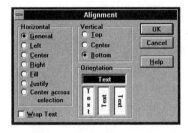

Fig. 5.4
The Alignment
dialog box.

3. In the Horizontal section, select General to align text to the left and numbers to the right. Select Left, Center, or Right to align text or numbers accordingly. Select Fill to fill the entire cell with the cell contents. Select the Wrap Text check box to make text wrap according to the width of the cell.

4. Choose OK or press ⏎Enter.

Exercise 2.1: Aligning Data and Text Using the Toolbar

In this exercise, you align text in a range, using the Toolbar. If you have not already done so, open the FIRST.XLS worksheet you created in Chapter 3.

1. Select the range B3:F3 by dragging over the cells with the cell pointer.

2. Click the Right-Align tool in the Toolbar to apply alignment formatting to the selection.

Exercise 2.2: Aligning Data and Text Using the Format Alignment Command

In this exercise, you align text in a range in the FIRST.XLS worksheet, using the Format Alignment command.

1. Select the range A5:A7 by dragging over the cells with the cell pointer.
2. Open the Format menu, and choose the Alignment command. The Alignment dialog box appears (see fig. 5.4).
3. In the Horizontal section, select the Right option button.
4. Choose OK or press ⏎Enter. The text is right-aligned.

Aligning Text To Wrap within a Cell

You can align text entries to wrap within a single cell or a range of cells. To wrap a string of text within a cell or range, follow these steps:

1. Select a cell or range, and enter the text.
2. Open the Format menu, and choose the Alignment command. The Alignment dialog box appears (see fig. 5.4).
3. Select the Wrap Text check box.
4. Choose OK or press ⏎Enter. The text is wrapped within the cell or range.

Exercise 2.3: Wrapping Text Using the Format Alignment Command

In this exercise, you wrap a string of text within a cell.

1. Select cell A9, and type the following text:

   This is the first Excel worksheet I created.

   Press ⏎Enter to enter the text into the cell. Notice that the text extends across other cells.
2. Open the Format menu, and choose the Alignment command. The Alignment dialog box appears (see fig. 5.4).
3. Click the Wrap Text check box so that an X appears in it.
4. Choose OK or press ⏎Enter.

122

Aligning Text To Center Over Columns

You can center text over a selected range of columns, using the Alignment tool on the Toolbar or using the Format Alignment command. To center text over multiple columns, follow these steps:

1. Select a cell, and enter the text.

2. Select the cell containing the text and the range of columns you would like to center the text across. (Selected cells defining the range of columns must be blank.)

Center Across Columns tool

Fig. 5.5
Centers selected text across columns.

5

3. Click the Center Across Columns tool on the Toolbar (see fig. 5.5).

   Or choose the Format Alignment command. The Alignment dialog box appears (see fig. 5.4). Select Center across selection in the Horizontal section, and then choose OK or press ⏎Enter. The text is centered across the selected columns.

Exercise 2.4: Centering Text over Multiple Columns Using the Toolbar

In this exercise, you center text over columns B through E, using the Toolbar.

1. Select cell B2, and type **CASHMAN, INC.** Press ⏎Enter to enter the text into the cell.

2. Select cell B2 and the range of columns you would like to center the text across (columns B through E) by dragging over the columns with the cell pointer.

3. Click the Center Across Columns tool on the Toolbar.

Aligning Text To Appear Vertical or Horizontal

Excel 4.0 enables you to format text to appear vertical or horizontal. When aligning text vertically or horizontally, you may need to use Excel's Best Fit function.

To format text to appear vertical or horizontal, follow these steps:

1. Select the text you want to format.

2. Open the Format menu, and choose the Alignment command. The Alignment dialog box appears (see fig. 5.4).

3. In the Orientation section of the dialog box, select the vertical or horizontal orientation you want.

4. If you selected a vertical orientation, also select a specific vertical alignment (Top, Center, or Bottom) in the Vertical section.

5. Choose OK or press ⏎Enter. The worksheet displays vertical or horizontal text orientation (see fig. 5.6).

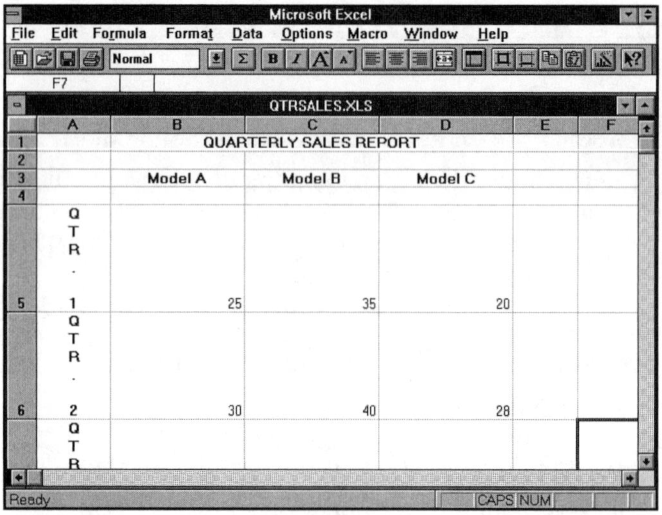

5

Fig. 5.6
Vertical text
orientation in
column A.

To quickly adjust the column width or row height, follow the steps for the Best Fit feature covered in Chapter 4's section "Objective 6: To Change Column Width and Row Height."

Exercise 2.5: Aligning Text To Appear Vertical

In this exercise, you format the text to be displayed vertically.

1. Select cell F3.

2. Open the Format menu, and choose the Alignment command. The Alignment dialog box appears (see fig. 5.4).

124

3. In the Vertical section of the dialog box, select the Center option.

4. In the Orientation section of the dialog box, click the far left rectangle.

5. Choose OK or press ⏎Enter .

Objective 3: To Change Fonts

Excel 4.0 enables you to use up to 256 fonts on a worksheet. With the Fonts dialog box, you can select a font type, choose a size for the selected font, and apply a font style. The list of fonts available in the Font dialog box depends on the type of printer you are using. If you want to increase or decrease the size of the font in a cell without actually changing the font type, use the Increase or Decrease font size tools. These tools are located in the middle of the Standard Toolbar. For example, to increase a font size, simply select the cell that contains the text you want to change, and click the Increase font size tool. Excel changes the font size.

To change a font, follow these steps:

1. Select a cell, a range, or the entire worksheet. (To select the entire worksheet, click in the area where the column and row headings intersect.)

2. Open the Format menu, and choose the Font command. The Font dialog box appears (see fig. 5.7).

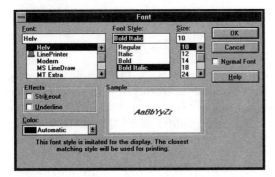

Fig. 5.7
The Font dialog box.

3. Select the options you want to apply. Select the type of font you want from the Font list. The sizes available for the selected font appear in the Size list; select the size you want, and select the style you want to apply (Bold, Italic, and so on) from the Font Style list. To display the

125

5

Color list, click the down arrow; use ↑ and ↓ to select a color from the list. Select the Strikeout and Underline check boxes in the Effects section if you want to apply these formats. The Sample area of the dialog box shows you what the selected options look like.

Note: Many fonts can be displayed on your screen but cannot be printed by your printer. If your printer cannot print a font that has been selected, it tries to match the font with the closest printer font available.

If the Normal Font check box is selected, the default font and size are applied to the selection.

4. Choose OK or press ⏎Enter to apply the formatting to the text.

Exercise 3.1: Changing the Font in a Range

In this exercise, you change the font in a range of cells. If you have not already done so, open the FIRST.XLS worksheet you created in Chapter 3.

1. Select the range A3:E3.

2. Open the Format menu, and choose the Font command. The Font dialog box appears (see fig. 5.7).

3. In the Font dialog box, select the Terminal font, Bold Italic style, size 10, and the color Magenta.

4. Choose OK or press ⏎Enter to apply the formatting to the range.

Objective 4: To Justify Paragraphs

Although spreadsheet applications are not intended to handle word processing tasks, some users incorporate large text entries in worksheet cells. For those users, the Format Justify command is helpful. The Format Justify command enables you to select long text entries and spread the text over a selected area. The long text entries are easier to edit if they are organized as paragraphs in a defined area. To enter text into a cell that stretches over five columns and to confine this text to an area of three columns and three rows, follow these steps:

1. Select the cell or range containing the text, and select the columns and rows you want to define as the area for justification.

2. Open the Format menu, and choose the Justify command.

The selected text is divided to fill the defined area and appears justified (see fig. 5.8 and fig. 5.9).

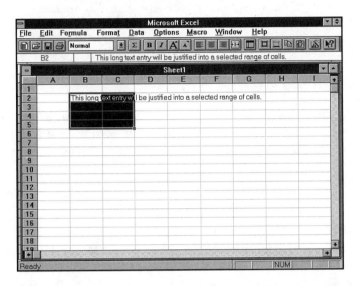

Fig. 5.8
Text before
justifying.

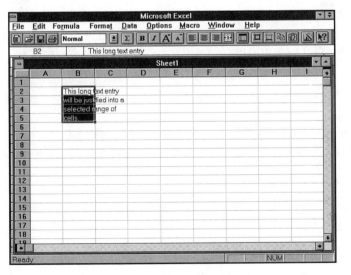

Fig. 5.9
Text after
justifying.

If the defined area is not large enough to hold the justified text, Excel displays an alert dialog box. If you choose OK, the text will extend beyond the defined area. If the text spills over into cells that contain text, the existing text will move down to accommodate the justified text. If the text spills over into cells that contain numbers or formulas, however, the text will overwrite the numbers or formulas in the cells. If you accidentally overwrite cells that contain numbers or formulas, choose the Edit Undo command immediately to reverse the Justification command.

Exercise 4.1: Justifying a Paragraph

For this exercise, start with an empty worksheet. You can close the worksheet you have been working on (FIRST.XLS), but don't save the formatting changes you have made. Choose the **File Close** command to close the worksheet. When the dialog box appears, choose **No**.

To enter text into a cell that stretches over five columns and to confine this text to an area of four columns and three rows, follow these steps:

1. Select cell B3, and type the following text:

   Andrew Cashman, the CEO of this firm, is responsible for this outstanding Annual Report.

   Press ⏎Enter to enter the text into the cell.

2. Select the range B3:E5.

3. Open the Format menu, and choose the Justify command. The selected text is confined to four columns and three rows.

Objective 5: To Format Cells

So far most of this chapter has dealt with formatting numbers or text. This section deals specifically with applying cell formats. Formatting cells includes adding a border around a cell or range of cells, filling a cell with a color or pattern, and automatically formatting a range.

To place borders around a cell or to place a single or double underline below a series of numbers, you use the Border dialog box.

To apply a border to a cell or selected range, follow these steps:

1. Select the cell or range you want to format.

2. Open the Format menu, and choose the Border command. The Border dialog box appears (see fig. 5.10).

128

Fig. 5.10
The Border dialog
box.

5

3. Choose the placement of the border by selecting Outline, Left, Right,
   Top, or Bottom in the Border section. The Outline option puts a
   border around the outer edges of the selection. The Left, Right, Top,
   and Bottom options put a border along the specified edges of each
   cell in the selection.

   From the Style section, select the type of border you want. To change
   the color of the border, choose the Color list by clicking the down
   arrow to display the list of colors. Select the Shade check box to make
   the selected cells shaded.

4. Choose OK or press ⏎Enter.

You can apply frequently used borders, such as an outline around a selected
cell or range, from the Toolbar. The Toolbar includes an Outline Border tool
and a Bottom Border tool. In fig. 5.11, cells B8 through D8 have a bottom
border.

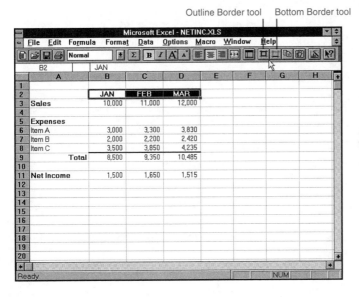

Fig. 5.11
A bottom border.

To apply a border using the Border tools, first select the cell or range you want to format, and then choose the Border tool. If you want a thin outline border to appear around the edges of the selected cell or range, choose the Outline Border tool. If you want a thin line border to appear on the bottom of a selected cell or of each row in a selected range, choose the Bottom Border tool.

In addition to adding borders to cells, you can enhance a cell with patterns and colors. The Format **P**atterns command enables you to choose foreground and background colors as well as a pattern from the Patterns dialog box.

To format a cell with colors and patterns, follow these steps:

1. Select the cell or range you want to format.

2. Open the Format menu, and choose the **P**atterns command. The Patterns dialog box appears (see fig. 5.12).

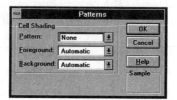

Fig. 5.12
The Patterns
dialog box.

3. Display the **P**attern drop-down list by clicking the down arrow. Follow the same procedure for displaying the **F**oreground color list and the **B**ackground color list. If the foreground and background colors are the same, the cell displays a solid color. The Sample box in the lower right corner of the dialog box shows you what the formatting looks like.

4. Choose OK or press ⏎Enter.

If you do not like the formatting you have chosen after it has been applied, select the Edit Undo formatting command before proceeding with another command. If you like the formatting and want to apply the same formatting to another area, select the new area and choose the **E**dit **R**epeat Patterns formatting command immediately after the formatting has been applied.

Exercise 5.1: Formatting a Range of Cells

In this exercise, you apply a border to a range. Open the FIRST.XLS worksheet you created in Chapter 3.

130

1. Select the range A3:F3.

2. Open the Format menu, and choose the Border command. The Border dialog box appears (see fig. 5.10).

3. Choose the placement of the border by selecting Outline in the Border section. Select the thickness of the border by clicking the thickest solid line in the Style section. To change the color of the border, display the Color list by clicking the down arrow, and then select Red. Click the Shade check box to make the selected cells shaded.

4. Choose OK or press ⏎Enter.

5. Click a cell outside the range A3:F3 to see the change.

Using Automatic Range Formatting

If you aren't sure which colors and formats work well together, Excel's AutoFormat feature will eliminate much of the work for you. AutoFormat enables you to select from 14 predefined range formats. These formats are a combination of number formats, cell alignments, column widths, row heights, fonts, borders, and other formatting options. Automatic formatting can be applied by using the Format AutoFormat command or by using the AutoFormat tool on the Toolbar.

To automatically format a range, follow these steps:

1. Select the range you want to format.

2. Open the Format menu, and choose the AutoFormat command. The AutoFormat dialog box appears.

3. From the Table Format list box, select one of the 14 format types. In the Sample box, Excel displays the selected format (see fig. 5.13).

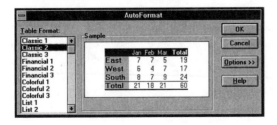

Fig. 5.13
The selected format displayed in the Sample box.

4. Choose OK or press ⏎Enter. Predefined formatting is applied to the selected range.

You also can use the Toolbar to apply automatic formatting. The AutoFormat tool cycles through each of the predefined formats and applies the format to the selected range (see fig. 5.14).

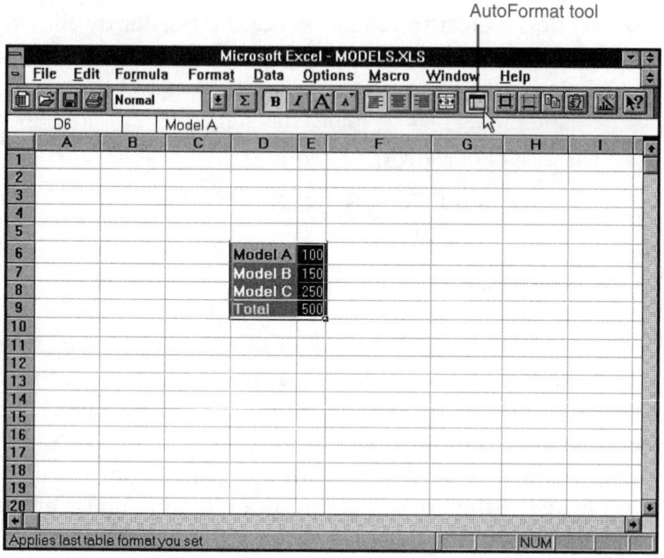

AutoFormat tool

Fig. 5.14
Using the
AutoFormat tool
to apply pre-
defined format-
ting to a range.

Exercise 5.2: Using the Format AutoFormat Command

In this exercise, you format a range automatically in the FIRST.XLS worksheet, using the Format AutoFormat command.

1. Select the range A3:F7.
2. Open the Format menu, and choose the AutoFormat command. The AutoFormat dialog box appears (see fig. 5.13).
3. Select Financial 3 from the Table Format list box.
4. Choose OK or press ⏎Enter.
5. Click a cell outside the range to see the change.

Using the Toolbar

The Standard Toolbar in Excel 4.0 contains tools that represent commonly used commands such as Bold, Italic, and Center (see fig. 5.15).

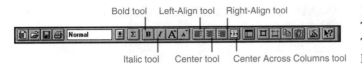

Fig. 5.15
The Standard
Toolbar in
Excel 4.0.

In previous sections of this chapter, you learned that you can apply bold or italic formatting to text or numbers using the Format Font command. A much faster way to accomplish this task is to use the Toolbar. Select the cells you want to format, and choose the Bold tool to boldface the selection, or the Italic tool to italicize the selection. If the formatting is turned on, the tool on the Toolbar changes color. If you decide that you do not want the formatting, select the tool again. The formatting turns off, and the icon returns to its normal color.

Objective 6: To Check Spelling

Spelling is a new function in Excel 4.0 that enables you to check worksheets, macro sheets, and charts for spelling errors, and to correct the original text quickly. The spell checker in the Options menu offers a standard dictionary and a customized dictionary from which you can check for misspelled words. Excel displays misspelled words, repeated words in a single cell, and words that might not display a normal pattern of capitalization. You can spell check the entire worksheet, a single word, or a defined range. If you do not select a word or range of words, Excel checks the spelling for all text in the worksheet, including headers, footers, foot notes, annotations, and hidden text.

To use the spell checker, follow these steps:

1. Select cell A1 to begin spell checking from the beginning of the worksheet. Spell checking starts from the point of the active cell and moves forward to the end of the worksheet. If you do not start spell checking in cell A1, a dialog box will prompt you to continue spell checking from the beginning.

2. Open the Options menu, and choose the Spelling command. The Spelling dialog box appears, and Excel begins checking for misspelled words, repeated words, and unusual capitalization (see fig. 5.16).

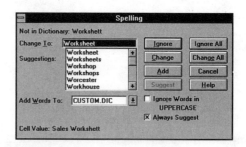

Fig. 5.16
The Spelling
dialog box.

Each time a word appears in the dialog box, you can choose to ignore the word, ignore all identical words found throughout the worksheet, change the word, change all identical words found throughout the worksheet, or add the word to a dictionary.

3. To substitute the misspelled word with the word suggested in the Change To text box, choose the Change button. To change all examples of the same word found throughout the entire worksheet, choose the Change All button.

4. To use a different correction, select a word from the Suggestions list box and choose the Change or Change All button. If Excel cannot suggest an alternative word, the misspelled word appears in the Change To text box. You can ignore the word by choosing the Ignore button; or you can type a new word in the Change To text box, and then choose the Change button.

  • To leave a word unchanged, choose the Ignore button. To leave the word unchanged throughout the entire worksheet, select Ignore All.

  • To delete a repeated word, choose the Change button. Excel removes the repeated word and the unnecessary spaces between the remaining words.

  • To add a word to the dictionary, choose the Add button.

  • To clear the dialog box, choose OK or press [Esc].

5. If you did not begin the spell check with cell A1 as the active cell, a dialog box prompts you to continue spell checking from the beginning. Choose Yes to continue checking from the beginning of the worksheet to the point where the spell checking began.

Exercise 6.1: Spell Checking Your Worksheet

In this exercise, you use the spell checker on the FIRST.XLS worksheet. You begin by entering a misspelled word that the spell checker can find.

1. To put in a misspelled word, make cell F3 the active cell, type TOTL, and press ⏎Enter.
2. Select cell A1 to begin spell checking from the beginning of the worksheet.
3. Open the Options menu, and choose the Spelling command.
4. When the spell checker questions the spelling QTR, click the Ignore button.
5. When the spell checker finds TOTL misspelled, scroll down the Suggestions list box until TOTAL appears. Click TOTAL to select it. TOTAL appears in the Change To text box.
6. To replace the misspelled word with TOTAL, choose the Change button.

5

Summary

This chapter covered the commands and features that enable you to improve the appearance of your worksheets. You learned about number formats, including date and time formats. You learned how to format commands with the AutoFormat feature, center text over columns, align vertical and horizontal text, change fonts, and apply justification. You also learned how to apply a style, using the Style menu on the Toolbar. Finally, you learned how to check for misspellings in your worksheet.

The next chapter introduces you to Excel's Formula Paste Function command. This command enables you to access a list of over 150 built-in functions. Functions are predefined formulas that can save considerable time and increase accuracy in a worksheet requiring specific calculations. Chapter 6, "Using Functions," explains what a function is, the various types of functions, and what some of the built-in functions do.

Testing Your Knowledge

True/False Questions

1. If you want dollar signs or commas to appear in the numbers in your worksheet, you must type them in as you enter each number in a cell.

2. The Normal format on the Style menu is the same as Excel's default format.

3. If you type 7–10–95 in a cell, Excel will subtract the three numbers.

4. A tool in the Standard Toolbar enables you to italicize text in a worksheet.

5. You can underline the contents of a cell by using the Border command in the Format menu.

Multiple Choice Questions

1. The spell checker is accessed from the _____ menu.
   - A. Help
   - B. Format
   - C. Window
   - D. Options

2. Which of the following correctly refers to the range of cells from A5 to E5?
   - A. A5–E5
   - B. A5:E5
   - C. A5>E5
   - D. none of these answers

3. Which alignment is the Excel default for numbers in cells?
   - A. left
   - B. center
   - C. right
   - D. wrap

4. Which term is used to refer to the size and shape of characters in the worksheet?
   - A. font
   - B. scale
   - C. fill
   - D. pixel

5. Which alignment is the Excel default for text in cells?
   - A. left
   - B. center
   - C. right
   - D. wrap

Fill-in-the-Blank Questions

1. The left, right, and center Alignment tools are located in the
   _____.
2. To display text vertically, you choose the _____ command in the
   Format menu.
3. The Format _____ command enables you to select long text
   entries and spread the text over a selected area.
4. You can use the _____ tool on the Toolbar to center text in a
   cell.
5. You can change the appearance of text, numbers, or cells in a
   worksheet by using a _____ command.

Review: Short Projects

1. Using the Format AutoFormat Command

   Open the grading worksheet, C4PROJ2.XLS, which you built in the
   short projects in Chapter 4. Use the Format AutoFormat command to
   apply the Classic 2 format to your worksheet. Print the worksheet.
   Then use the Format AutoFormat command to apply the Colorful 2
   format to your worksheet.

2. Using the Format Tools and Format Border Command

   Open the original grading worksheet, C4PROJ2.XLS. Use the Increase
   font size tool to increase the font size of the column headings. Use the
   Bold tool to darken the headings. Use the Format Border command to
   underline the column headings with a thick blue line.

3. More Formatting and a Spelling Check

   In the C4PROJ2.XLS worksheet, use the Decrease font size tool twice
   to reduce the size of the column headings. Then center the headings
   over each column. Use the Format Number command to display all the
   grades with two decimal places. Use the spell checker to check for
   misspellings in the worksheet. Are names always identified as possible
   misspellings?

Review: Long Projects

1. Preparing a Worksheet for a Presentation

   Open the NSCC COMPANY QUARTERLY REPORT worksheet,
   C4LP1.XLS, which you created in the first long project at the end of

5

Chapter 4. Do not use the AutoFormat feature in this project. Change the font type and size of the text in the title. Try to center the title between the left and right edges of the worksheet. Place borders around the column headings, and select a pattern to use inside the cells of the column headings. Use the Format Borders command to display thick vertical lines between the cells in rows 4 through 17. Format all numbers in the worksheet as currency with two decimal places. Display negative numbers in red. Place the date in cell A1. Save the worksheet as C5LP1.XLS, and print the worksheet.

2. Completing the International Investments Worksheet

Open the financial worksheet, C4LP2.XLS, which you created in the second long project at the end of Chapter 4. Insert three rows at the top of the worksheet, and enter the title CONSOLIDATED UNIVERSAL AMALGAMATED HOLDING COMPANY INCORPORATED LIMITED in cell C1. Then use the Format Justify command to place this title in rows 1 through 3 of columns C through F. Align the (Mil.) column headings vertically in their cells. Apply the Financial 2 AutoFormat to the worksheet, and then spell check the worksheet. Save the worksheet as C5LP2.XLS, and print the worksheet.

Using Functions

6

Excel was designed with more than 150 built-in formulas called *functions*. A function is a predefined formula that performs calculations on data in your worksheet. When you use a function, you do not have to enter mathematical operators as you do in a formula. In many cases, functions not only save you time but also increase the accuracy of the results. You can insert a function into a formula or into another function.

A calculation may sometimes involve so many cells or groups of cells that typing formulas and selecting cells may prove cumbersome and inaccurate. For example, you may need to total 50 cells; it would take quite a while to type the correct formula to perform this calculation. However, with the SUM function, it is easy to total a column or row of 50 cells. And if constructing your own formula becomes too complicated, Excel already may have a function that will accomplish your goal.

In this chapter, you will learn what a function is and how to enter a function. You also will learn about the different types of functions.

Objectives

1. To Understand What a Function Is
2. To Enter a Function
3. To Recognize the Types of Functions

Key Terms in This Chapter	
Function	A predefined formula consisting of a name and arguments
Argument	The data a function acts upon to produce a result
Serial number	A date expressed as a number. Days are numbered from the beginning of the 20th century. January 1, 1900, is day number one; 1/25/1900 is the date serial number 25, and so on.
Array	A range of values or formulas treated as one group
Annuity calculations	Calculations based on a series of even payments over a specified time

6

Objective 1: To Understand What a Function Is

As stated in the introduction to this chapter, a function is a predefined formula that consists of the function's name and arguments. An *argument* is the selected or entered data the function acts upon to produce a result. An argument can be a single cell reference, a group of cells, or a number. Some functions require a single argument; others require multiple arguments. The function name is preceded by an equal sign (=) and followed by an argument or a series of arguments. Function arguments are enclosed in parentheses, and arguments are separated by a comma. The formula bar in fig. 6.1 displays a simple function that adds a list of numbers, using the SUM function.

The argument in the function is the range of cells B6 to B8. The result of this function is the sum of the values in cells B6 through B8. As with a formula, the result of a function appears in the cell that contains the function (cell B9). The function appears in the formula bar. This function contains one argument. Other functions, however, may contain several arguments, and some functions have no arguments.

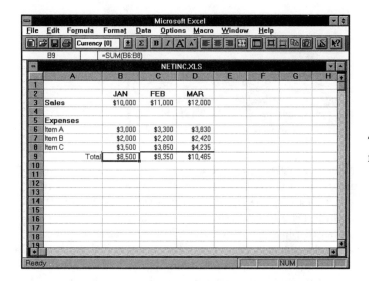

Fig. 6.1
The SUM
function.

6

Objective 2: To Enter a Function

There are two ways to enter a function into the active cell. The first way is to actually type in the function name and arguments. For example, you type = (the equal sign), followed by the function name **SUM**, followed by an open (left) parenthesis. Then you enter the cell or range of cells you want the function to use as its argument. End the function with a close (right) parenthesis, and then press ⏎Enter. The second way to enter a function in an active cell is to use the Paste Function command in the Formula menu. This method automatically inserts the elements required for using a function.

If you have not used a function before, the Formula Paste Function method is probably the best way to enter the function. When you type a function, you can make a mistake such as forgetting a comma or an argument. But when you use the Formula Paste Function command, Excel pastes the function and also pastes argument placeholders to remind you of the arguments necessary to complete the function properly. If you want, you can turn off the Argument Paste option by clicking the Paste Arguments check box in the Paste Function dialog box (see fig. 6.2).

Fig. 6.2
The Paste Func-
tion dialog box,
in which you
select and enter
a function.

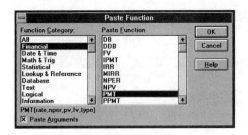

When you choose the Formula Paste Function command, the Paste Function dialog box appears, displaying a Function Category list and a Paste Function list. The Function Category list displays the major function types. Some of these function types include Date & Time, Financial, Math & Trig, and Statistical. The Paste Function list displays the set of functions within the selected function category. If you select Date & Time from the Function Category, all the Date & Time paste functions are displayed alphabetically in the Paste Function list box (for example, hour, minute, and month). Both the Function Category and Paste Function lists are alphabetically sensitive. If you press the first letter of the function name you want to access, the first function name beginning with that letter is selected. Use the scroll bar or ↑ and ↓ to scroll the list and select a function name.

To enter a function in the active cell using the Formula Paste Function command, follow these steps:

1. Select the cell in which you want to enter the function.

2. Open the Formula menu, and choose the Paste Function command. The Paste Function dialog box appears (see fig. 6.2).

   The Paste Arguments option is turned on by default (notice the X in the Paste Arguments check box). This option displays temporary argument placeholders in the formula bar to remind you of the information needed to complete the function. If you want placeholders to appear in parentheses following the function name in the formula bar, make sure that the Paste Arguments check box contains an X.

3. Select the Function Category you want, and then select the function you want to use from the Paste Function list box.

4. Choose OK or press ↵Enter. The function appears in the formula bar. If the Paste Argument option is turned on, you will see that the first argument placeholder inside the parentheses is selected. Replace the argument placeholder with the required data by typing the actual argument. Select the other argument placeholders (double-click

them). Then replace the placeholders by typing the data or selecting the worksheet cell(s) that contain the data for the actual arguments.

5. After the function is complete, select the check mark box in the formula bar or press ⏎Enter. The result of the function appears in the cell. The function appears in the formula bar. If you want to edit the function, press F2 or click in the formula bar.

Exercise 2.1: Entering a Function By Typing

For this exercise, open the calorie count worksheet (C3LP1.XLS) you created in the first long project in Chapter 3. In the following steps, you type a function that will total a range of cells in the worksheet.

1. Make cell D14 the active cell.

2. Type =SUM(B10:H10), and press ⏎Enter. Do not put spaces in the function as you type.

3. Compare the result with the result in cell D12 to verify that the formula and the function produce the same results.

Exercise 2.2: Entering a Function Using the Formula Paste Function Command

In this exercise, you enter a function using the Formula Paste Function command in your calorie count worksheet.

1. Make cell D16 the active cell.

2. Open the Formula menu, and choose the Paste Function command. The Paste Function dialog box appears (see fig. 6.2).

3. Select the Statistical category in the Function Category list box.

4. Select the AVERAGE function in the Paste Function list box. Notice that the Paste Arguments check box is selected.

5. Choose OK or press ⏎Enter.

6. The AVERAGE function appears in the formula bar with argument placeholders.

7. Type B6:, and then press Del to remove the comma between placeholders. Remember—no spaces should appear in the function.

8. Position the I-beam pointer on the number2 placeholder and double-click.

6

9. Type H6, and then press [Del] four times to remove the comma and ellipses.

10. Press [↵Enter].

11. Verify with your calculator that you have averaged daily total calories correctly.

Exercise 2.3: Entering a Function Using the Formula Paste Function Command without Using Argument Placeholders

In this exercise, you enter a function using the Formula Paste Function command in your calorie count worksheet. This time you do not use argument placeholders.

1. Make cell D18 the active cell.

2. Open the Formula menu, and choose the Paste Function command.

3. Select the Statistical category in the Function Category list box.

4. Select the AVERAGE function in the Paste Function list box. Notice that the Paste Arguments check box is selected.

5. Click the Paste Arguments check box to remove the X and turn off the option.

6. Choose OK or press [↵Enter].

7. The AVERAGE function appears in the formula bar without argument placeholders.

8. Type B6:H6. Remember—no spaces should appear in the function.

9. Press [↵Enter].

Pasting arguments may seem like more trouble than help in the above exercises. This is not the case, however, with many of the Financial functions discussed below. As you become familiar with the types of functions, you will realize when you need placeholder reminders and when you don't.

Some functions do not require an argument. For example the NOW( ) function places the current date and time in a cell, and an argument is not required. Some functions require only one argument, and some functions require several arguments. Most functions have a limit of 14 arguments (although you rarely use that many). If an argument can be repeated, ellipses (...) follow the argument name, indicating that the argument can be repeated up to the limit. If a function uses multiple arguments, commas separate the arguments.

144

If multiple argument placeholders appear in parentheses and you need only one set of data for the argument, you can delete the remaining placeholders inside the parentheses. For example, in =SUM(number1, number2...), you could select the placeholder number1 and enter the range B6:B8 for the argument. Then, because you wouldn't need the argument number2, you would delete it from the formula bar before pressing Enter. Otherwise, you would get an error message.

One of the most common errors when you enter a function is leaving out a comma between arguments. Another mistake is inserting spaces in the function. Do not put spaces anywhere in the function. If you need to edit a function, activate the formula bar by pressing [F2] or clicking in the formula bar. Use normal editing procedures to make insertions or deletions. In some cases, if you have an error in your function, a message dialog box appears. The message prompts you to correct the error in the formula bar. Choose OK or press [⏎Enter] to clear the error message dialog box. The part of the function causing the error is selected in the formula bar. You then can determine what the error might be. Check for mistakes such as missing commas, too many commas, or blank spaces in the selected area.

When you enter a function and choose the Paste Arguments option, the argument placeholders do not indicate which arguments are mandatory and which ones are optional. This chapter gives a brief description of some of the most commonly used worksheet functions and lists the arguments for each function. The optional arguments are italicized. A complete listing of all the functions is available in Excel's Help.

When you use the Formula Paste Function command, the Paste Arguments option increases your efficiency and accuracy when you enter the function. First, the option reminds you of the necessary arguments, so you are less likely to have an argument missing in the function. Second, the option enables you to easily select the argument placeholder and replace it without having to worry about deleting a comma. You can use the mouse or the keyboard to select an argument placeholder. To select an argument placeholder using the keyboard, position the cursor at the beginning of the placeholder, hold down [⇧Shift] and use [→]. After the argument placeholder is selected, you can replace it by typing in the data or cell reference, or by selecting a cell or range in the worksheet containing the data. Table 6.1 lists the types of arguments and the descriptions.

6

Table 6.1 Function Argument Types	
Argument Type	*Description*
Value	A number or cell reference containing a value
Logical	Result if formula is TRUE or FALSE
Number	A number or numeric formula
Text	Nonnumeric data; text must be enclosed in quotation marks
Array	A range of values treated as a single group
Serial number	A date and time
Reference	A cell or range address

6

Objective 3: To Recognize the Types of Functions

Excel has more than 150 built-in functions. Most of these functions are grouped into one of the following categories:

Date & Time

Engineering

Financial

Information

Logical

Lookup & Reference

Math & Trig

Statistical

Text

A complete listing of all the functions and a short explanation of each function is available under the Worksheet Functions topic in Excel's Help. If you need more information on the function, click the function's name in the list. You will be given an explanation of the function and examples of its use.

Date & Time Functions

To keep track of the date and time, Excel counts the number of days that have passed since the beginning of the 20th century. Excel uses a date serial number that starts with January 1, 1900, as day number 1. All days from this date forward are numbered sequentially. For example, if you used a date function to find the serial number for July 4, 1991, the serial number returned is 33423 (the number of days that have passed, by that date, since January 1, 1900). Excel also includes date functions for converting the day, month, year, and time to serial numbers. You also can use functions to convert a serial number to the actual date or time.

The date and time cell formats that were discussed in Chapter 5 are designed to be used with the date and time functions so that you have complete control over the appearance of dates and times in your worksheet. When a date function is used in a cell, the cell's format is automatically changed from General, which is the default, to a date format. To see the actual serial number of a date, you would use the DATE function in a cell, and then change the format of the cell back to General.

The functions TODAY and NOW enable you to use the current date or the current date and time, respectively. The NOW function is useful for documents that must always include the current date and time. If you use the NOW function, you do not need to change the date on a worksheet each time you print it. Some of the date and time functions are listed in table 6.2.

Table 6.2 Date & Time Functions	
Function	*Description*
DATE(year,month,day)	Returns specified date
DATEVALUE(date_text)	Returns date text
DAY(serial_number)	Returns day, as an integer from 1 to 31, corresponding to serial number
DAYS360(start_date,end_date)	Returns number of days between two dates
HOUR(serial_number)	Returns hour, as an integer from 0 to 23, corresponding to serial number

continues

Table 6.2 Continued	
Function	*Description*
MINUTE(serial_number)	Returns minute, as an integer from 0 to 59, corresponding to serial number
MONTH(serial_number)	Returns month, as an integer from 1 to 12, corresponding to serial number
NETWORKDAYS (start_date,end_date,holidays)	Returns the number of whole working days between start_date and end_date; working days exclude weekends and any dates identified in holidays
NOW( )	Returns serial number of current date and time
SECOND(serial_number)	Returns second, as an integer from 1 to 59, corresponding to serial number
TIME(hour,minute,second)	Returns serial number of time specified by hour, minute, and second
TODAY( )	Returns serial number of current date
WORKDAY(start_date,days,*holidays*)	Returns the serial number date that is the indicated number of working days before or after start_date; working days exclude weekends and any dates identified in *holidays*
YEAR(serial_number)	Returns year corresponding to serial number

6

Exercise 3.1: Entering a Date Function in a Cell

In this exercise, you enter a date function in a cell. Choose the File New Worksheet command to display an empty worksheet.

1. Make cell A1 the active cell.
2. Open the Formula menu, and choose the Paste Function command.
3. Select Date & Time in the Function Category list box.
4. Select NOW in the Paste Function list box.
5. Choose OK or press ⏎Enter. Notice that the function is in the formula bar.
6. Press ⏎Enter.
7. Widen column A so that its width is 12. The date and time are displayed (assuming your computer has the time and date set properly).
8. Change the format of cell A1 to Number General as you learned in Chapter 5. The number you see is the serial number of the date and time.
9. Change the format of cell A1 to the m/d/yy date format. You should see the date.

Engineering Functions

Excel 4.0 adds 22 new engineering functions to its comprehensive list of functions. Engineering functions include four Bessel functions and multiple BIN, DEC, and HEX functions to convert numbers from one type to another. To use the engineering functions, you must install one of the macro add-in files. For information about installing add-ins, refer to Excel's user guide.

Financial Functions

Excel has built-in financial functions that calculate payments on a loan, depreciation, present and future values, internal rate of returns, net present value, and other annuity calculations. An annuity function performs a calculation based on a series of even payments over a specified time. The factors involved in solving most annuity problems are PV (present value) or FV (future value), NPER (number of periods), PMT (payment each period), and RATE (periodic interest rate). These are all available as functions in Excel.

The Formula =PMT(0-1/12,360,250000) determines the monthly payment on a mortgage of $250,000, over a 30-year period at an annual interest rate of 10 per-cent. The arguments for the PMT function are nper, rate, pv, fv, and type. Type and future value are optional arguments. The number of periods in the argu-ment is 360, which is the total number of months for the loan. The peri-odic in-terest rate is the annual interest rate divided by 12; the interest rate must be in months because the payments are in months. The present value is the amount of the loan. The result of this function is $2,193.93 per month. Because this is an outflow of cash, the number appears in the cell as a negative number.

Type and FV are optional arguments and are not included in this calculation. (Optional arguments are italicized in this book.) Type can be 0 or 1. Zero as-sumes the cash flow is at the end of the period. One assumes the cash flow is at the beginning of the period. If no type is entered, zero is assumed. FV is the value at the end of the period. Table 6.3 lists some of the financial functions.

6

Table 6.3 Financial Functions	
Function	*Description*
ACCRINT(issue,first_interest, settlement,coupon,*par*,frequency, *basis*)	Accrued interest for a security that pays periodic interest
ACCRINTM(issue,settlement, *par*,*basis*)	Accrued interest for a rate, security that pays interest at maturity
CUMIPMT(rate,nper,pv, start_period,end_period,type)	Cumulative interest paid between start_period and end_period
CUMPRINC(rate,nper,pv, start_period,end_period,type)	Cumulative principal paid on a loan between start_period and end_period
DB(cost,salvage,life, period,*month*)	Real depreciation of an asset for a specific period using the fixed-declining balance method
DDB(cost,salvage,life, period, *factor*)	Double-declining balance method of depreciation if factor is 2 or omitted

150

Function	Description
DISC(settlement,maturity,pr, redemption,*basis*)	Discount rate for a security
EFFECT(nominal_rate,nper)	Effective annual interest rate
FV(rate,nper,pmt,pv,type)	Future value of an investment
FVSCHEDULE(principal,schedule)	Future value of an initial principal after applying a series of compound interest rates
IPMT(rate,per,nper,pv, *fv,type*)	Interest payment for a specified period
IRR(values, *guess*)	Internal rate of return for list of values
NPER(rate,pmt,pv, *fv,type*)	Number of periods for payments or investment
NPV(rate,value1,value2,...)	Net present value for list of values
PMT(rate,nper,pv, *fv,type*)	Periodic payment for an investment
PPMT(rate,per,nper,pv, *fv,type*)	Payment on the principal for a given period
PV(rate,nper,pmt, *fv,type*)	Present value of an investment
RATE(nper,pmt,pv,fv,type,guess)	Interest rate per period
SLN(cost,salvage,life)	Straight-line method of depreciation
SYD(cost,salvage,life,per)	Sum-of-years' method of depreciation
YIELD(settlement,maturity,rate, pr,redemption,frequency,*basis*)	Yield on a security that pays periodic interest

6

Exercise 3.2: Entering a Financial Function in a Cell

In this exercise, you use the PMT function. Assume that you borrow $15,000 at 9% interest for 3 years to buy a new car. What will your monthly payments be?

Choose the **File New Worksheet** command to display an empty worksheet.

1. Widen column A to 15. Make cell A1 the active cell.

2. Open the **Formula** menu, and choose the **Paste** Function command. The Paste Function dialog box appears (see fig. 6.2).

3. Select the Financial category from the Function Category list box.

4. Make sure that the Paste Arguments check box is selected. Then select the PMT function in the Paste Function list box, and choose OK or press ⏎Enter.

5. Type 0.09/12 for the rate placeholder (to convert annual to monthly interest rate).

6. Double-click the nper placeholder, and type 36 (the number of payment periods).

7. Double-click the pv placeholder, and type 15000 (the amount of the car loan).

8. Press Del to delete the remaining commas and the fv and type optional placeholders. Then press ⏎Enter.

9. The monthly payment of $477.00 should appear in red.

Information Functions

You can use Excel's built-in information functions to analyze cells, columns, rows, ranges, and areas. These parts of a worksheet may need to be analyzed before performing a calculation, function, or macro.

Excel includes nine IS functions in the information category. The IS functions enable you to test the type of entry in a cell or range; the functions return a logical value of TRUE or FALSE. If a cell meets the condition of the function, the value of the cell becomes TRUE. If the cell does not meet the function condition, the value is FALSE. For example, if you want to determine whether a cell is blank, you can use the ISBLANK function. If the cell is blank, the value is TRUE; otherwise, the value of the cell is FALSE. The IS functions are generally used with IF functions to establish the contents of a cell or range. In fig. 6.3, the two functions are combined to establish whether cell D10 contains text.

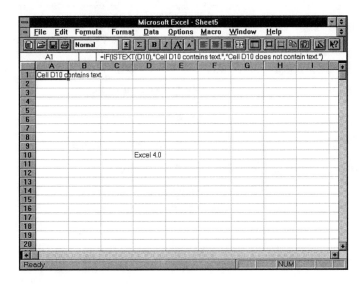

Fig. 6.3
The IF and
ISTEXT functions.

The IF and ISTEXT functions are entered as a combined function in cell A1. The IF function includes arguments to define value_if_true and value_if_false. The value_if_true argument is defined as a message, "Cell D10 contains text." The value_if_false argument is defined as a message, "Cell D10 does not contain text." If the result of the function in cell A1 is true (cell D10 does contain text), cell A1 displays the message Cell D10 contains text. If the result of the function in cell A1 is false (cell D10 does not contain text), cell A1 displays the message Cell D10 does not contain text. You must enter text arguments in quotation marks.

The other types of IS functions include ISBLANK, ISNONTEXT, and ISNUMBER. These functions are all described in Excel's Help.

Logical Functions

Excel's logical functions are used frequently for testing conditions and making decisions. The IF function enables you to set conditions. You can combine the IF function with other logical functions, such as AND and OR, to test for multiple conditions. Logical functions are listed and described in table 6.4.

153

Table 6.4 Logical Functions	
Function	*Description*
AND(logical1,*logical2*,...)	Returns TRUE if every argument is TRUE
FALSE( )	Returns logical value FALSE
IF(logical_test,value_if_true, *value_if_ false*)	Returns Value_if_true if logical test is TRUE; returns Value_if_false if logical value is FALSE
NOT(logical)	Reverses TRUE and FALSE logicals
OR(logical1,*logical2*,...)	Returns true if any argument is TRUE
TRUE( )	Returns logical value TRUE

6

Lookup & Reference Functions

Lookup functions are used to retrieve a value or cell reference from a table or an array in your worksheet. Examples of lookup functions include LOOKUP, MATCH, and various INDEX functions. Table 6.5 lists some of the lookup functions.

Table 6.5 Lookup & Reference Functions	
Function	*Description*
HLOOKUP(lookup_value,table_array, row_index_num)	Looks across the top row of range until value is met
LOOKUP(lookup_value,array)	Value in array selected by lookup value
VLOOKUP(lookup_value,table_array, col_index_num)	Looks down the first column of range until value is found

Math & Trig Functions

Excel's built-in mathematical functions enable you to perform standard arithmetic operations, including SUM and PRODUCT. Other mathematical

154

functions enable you to round and truncate numbers. These types of mathematical functions are the basis for using mathematical functions in building a worksheet.

Excel also includes several trigonometric functions, used primarily to build complex scientific and engineering formulas, and matrix functions, used primarily for solving complex problems that involve several unknown variables in an *array*, which is a rectangular range of values or formulas treated as a single group.

You can use three mathematical functions to round a number to certain specifications. The INT function rounds a number to the nearest integer. The TRUNC function truncates a number to its next lower integer, and the ROUND function rounds a number up or down. Some of the commonly used built-in mathematical functions are listed in table 6.6. For a complete list, see Excel's Help.

6

Table 6.6 Math & Trig Functions	
Function	*Description*
ABS(number)	Absolute value of number
COS(number)	Returns cosine of a number
INT(number)	Number rounded down to the nearest integer
PRODUCT(number1,*number2*,...)	Product of numbers
QUOTIENT(numerator,denominator)	Returns the integer portion of a division
RAND( )	Random number between 0 and 1
ROUND(number,num_digits)	Rounds number to specified number of digits
SIN(number)	Returns sine of a number
SQRT(number)	Square root of a number
SUM(number1,*number2*,...)	Total of arguments
TAN(number)	Returns tangent of a number
TRUNC(number,num_digits)	Changes number to an integer by truncating the decimal portion

Exercise 3.3: Entering a Math & Trig Function in a Cell

In this exercise, you take the square root of a number. Choose the File New Worksheet command to display an empty worksheet.

1. Make cell A10 the active cell.
2. Open the Formula menu, and choose the Paste Function command. The Paste Function dialog box appears (see fig. 6.2).
3. Select the Math & Trig category in the Function Category list box.
4. Scroll down the Paste Function list box until you see the SQRT function. Select SQRT, and turn off the Paste Arguments option.
5. Choose OK or press ↵Enter.
6. Type the number 68 as the argument of the function, and press ↵Enter.

Statistical Functions

Excel includes a comprehensive set of statistical functions. These functions enable you to find, for example, the average, minimum, maximum, standard deviation, or variance of a group of values in your worksheet. Many commonly used statistical tests—such as the T-test, Chi-Squared, and F-test—are available as functions. Other statistical functions include the TREND, LINEST, LOGEST, and GROWTH functions. You can use these functions to calculate lines and curves that fit data. Table 6.7 lists some of the most commonly used statistical functions built into Excel.

Table 6.7 Statistical Functions	
Function	*Description*
AVERAGE(number1,*number2,...*)	Returns average of defined range
CHITEST(actual_range,expected_range)	Returns the test for independence; returns the value from the chi-squared (c2) distribution for the statistic and the appropriate degrees of freedom

Function	Description
COUNTA(value1,*value2*,...)	Returns total of nonblank cells in range
FORECAST(x,known_y's,known_x's)	Returns a predicted value for x based on a linear regression of known x- and y-arrays or ranges of data
FREQUENCY(data_array,bins_array)	Returns a frequency distribution as a vertical array
FTEST(array1,array2)	Returns the results of an F-test
MAX(number1,*number2*,...)	Returns largest number in defined range
MEDIAN(number1,number2,...)	Returns middle value in defined range
MIN(number1,*number2*,...)	Returns smallest number in defined range
MODE(number1,*number2*,...)	Returns the most frequently occurring value in an array or range of data
PEARSON(array1,array2)	Returns the Pearson product moment correlation coefficient, r, a dimensionless index that ranges from -1.0 to 1.0 inclusive, and reflects the extent of a linear relationship between two data sets
PERCENTILE(array,k)	Returns the value from array at the k-th percentile
RSQ(known_y's,known_x's)	Returns the r2 value of the linear regression line through data points in known_y's and known_x's
STDEV(number1,*number2*,...)	Returns standard deviation for sample population

6

continues

157

Table 6.7 Continued	
Function	*Description*
STDEVP(number1,*number2,...*)	Returns standard deviation of entire population
STEYX(known_y's,known_x's)	Returns the standard error of the regression
TDIST(x,degrees_freedom,tails)	Returns the Student's t-distribution
VAR(number1,number2,...)	Returns variance for sample population
VARP(number1,number2,...)	Returns variance for entire population

Exercise 3.4: Entering a Statistical Function in a Cell

In this exercise, you enter a statistical function in the calorie count worksheet (C3LP1.XLS). Make sure that the worksheet is open.

1. Make cell A15 the active cell.
2. Type =**MAX(B6:H6)**, and press ⏎Enter. This function finds the largest number of daily calories consumed during the week.

Text Functions

Excel includes a number of built-in text functions that help you find or edit text in a cell or range. Several of these functions are listed in table 6.8.

Table 6.8 Text Functions	
Function	*Description*
LOWER(text)	Changes text to all lowercase
PROPER(text)	Changes text to lowercase with first character capitalized

Function	Description
TEXT(value,format_text)	Converts number value to formatted text value
UPPER(text)	Changes text to all uppercase
VALUE(text)	Converts text to number

Exercise 3.5: Entering a Text Function in a Cell

In this exercise, you enter a text function in a cell. Make sure that the C3LP1.XLS worksheet is open.

1. Make cell A18 the active cell.
2. Type =**LOWER(A12)**, and press ⏎Enter.

Because cell A12 contains TOTAL CALORIE DEFICIT =, cell A18 will contain the same text in lower case.

Summary

In this chapter, you were introduced to functions. You learned what a function is and how to use functions to improve accuracy and efficiency in formulas. You also learned what an argument is and how to paste functions and argument placeholders.

This chapter provided several tables outlining the different types of functions and what each function does. The tables provided you with the arguments that are necessary to produce a result using a function. Excel's Help contains a complete reference for all Excel functions.

Chapter 7, "Printing a Worksheet," deals with various aspects of printing. The chapter introduces you to the Excel commands for setting up the printer, previewing a document before it is printed, and adjusting margins and columns in Preview mode. You will learn how to define a print area, change the printer orientation, and create headers and footers for a document.

Testing Your Knowledge

True/False Questions

1. A function cannot be used inside a formula or another function.
2. Functions can be entered into a cell by using the Formula Paste Function command.
3. If a function uses multiple arguments, the arguments are separated with a colon.
4. When you use the Paste Arguments option, the argument placeholders indicate which arguments are optional.
5. The serial number for a day begins with January 1st of the current year.

Multiple Choice Questions

1. Which function would return the serial number of today's date?
   A. DATE
   B. DAY
   C. DATEVALUE
   D. none of these answers
2. Which function could be used to calculate your monthly payments for a new car?
   A. COST
   B. IRR
   C. PMT
   D. RATE
3. Which of the following functions is a math and trig function?
   A. SQRT
   B. MAX
   C. AVG
   D. VALUE

4. The year 1900 was a leap year (366 days). What would be the serial number for January 10, 1902?

    A. 10

    B. 741

    C. 1912

    D. none of these answers

5. Which of the following functions could be used in accounting to calculate the depreciation of equipment?

    A. DDB

    B. FV

    C. STDEVP

    D. VALUE

6

Fill-in-the-Blank Questions

1. A _____ is a predefined formula.

2. In a function, the _____ appears inside parentheses.

3. In the Paste Function dialog box, the Function _____ list box displays the major function types.

4. To select an argument placeholder that is displayed in the formula bar, place the I-beam pointer on the placeholder name and _____.

5. A complete explanation of all the functions available in Excel is found in Excel's _____.

Review: Short Projects

1. Using Time and Date Functions

   Open the FIRST.XLS worksheet, and place today's date (only) in cell G1. Widen column G if necessary. Place the time of day (only hours and minutes) in cell H1. Print the worksheet.

2. Calculating the Average

   In cell G5 of the FIRST.XLS worksheet, use a statistical function to calculate the average quarterly sales for the EAST region.

3. Calculating Monthly Payments

   Use the PMT function to calculate the monthly payments for borrowing $200,000 at 10% for 30 years.

Review: Long Projects

1. Using Date and Serial Numbers

   In an empty worksheet, use the serial number of today's date and the date formats to calculate what the dates will be 30, 60, and 90 days from today. (*Tip:* You can add numbers to a date serial number.) Print out today's date, and the dates 30, 60, and 90 days from today. Calculate the total number of days from the day that you were born until today. (*Tip:* Serial numbers of dates can be subtracted.)

2. Using Statistical Functions

   Open the financial worksheet (C4LP2.XLS) you created in the second long project at the end of Chapter 4. Use the statistical functions to determine the average, standard deviation, median, smallest value, and largest value for the SALES data. Perform the same calculations for the data in the NET INCOME column, for the data in the ASSETS column, and for the data in the MARKET VALUE column. (*Tip:* You can copy functions just as you copy formulas.) Label each of the statistics clearly. Save the worksheet as C6LP2.XLS, and print the worksheet.

6

Printing a Worksheet

Excel 4.0 has many features for viewing and printing a worksheet or chart (charts are discussed in the next chapter). Using Excel's Zoom command, you can view your worksheet at different levels of magnification. This capability enables you to reduce the size of your worksheet so that you can see more of it on-screen. Or you can enlarge an area of your worksheet so that you can format it more precisely. Using Excel's Print commands, you can enhance your worksheet or chart for an impressive presentation by customizing the appearance of the printout.

This chapter covers the steps involved when you use Excel's Zoom features and Print commands. In this chapter, you will learn how to define a print area, set up the page for printing, and preview before printing. Many of the commands in this chapter are only available if you have a printer attached to your computer. Most of the exercises require that you have a printer attached, and that it is set up for use with Windows.

Objectives

1. To Use the Zoom Command
2. To Set Up the Page
3. To Preview a Document
4. To Print a Document

Key Terms in This Chapter	
Default setting	Predefined settings that control the way all documents are printed
Portrait orientation	Prints your worksheet so that the data in the worksheet's columns prints vertically down the length of the page. Data rows print across the (8.5") width of the page. This is the Excel default.
Landscape orientation	Rotates the worksheet you see on-screen and prints it "sideways" so that the rows print vertically down the length of the page. This orientation fits more columns of a worksheet on one page.
Header	Text, date, page numbering, and formatting in the top margin of each page of a document
Footer	Text, date, page numbering, and formatting in the bottom margin of each page of a document
Print area	Defined section to be printed
Manual page break	Determines the end of a page; inserted with a command
Preview mode	Overview of the print area that shows you what the page will look like when printed

7

Objective 1: To Use the Zoom Command

Excel's Zoom command enables you to select varying levels of magnification or reduction in which to view your worksheet. This reduction capability is useful when you want to see more of a worksheet on-screen. Magnifying an area of the worksheet enables you to polish your formatting before you print. You can view the worksheet in increments varying from 10% to 400%. Five preset Zoom levels also exist. The Zoom command does not affect the way your worksheet prints; it only affects what you see on your screen. Table 7.1 describes the Window Zoom options.

164

Table 7.1 Window Zoom Options	
Option	*Description*
200%	Magnifies view to 200% of detail
100%	Displays normal view
75%	Reduces view to 75%
50%	Reduces view to 50%
25%	Reduces view to 25%
Fit Selection	Calculates Zoom factor so that all cells fit in current window size
Custom %	Enables you to choose level of magnification or reduction

To change the level of magnification on a worksheet, follow these steps:

1. Open the Window menu, and choose the Zoom command. The Zoom dialog box appears (see fig. 7.1).

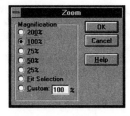

Fig. 7.1
The Zoom dialog box.

2. Select one of the preset Zoom sizes; or select the Custom option, and manually enter a Zoom factor.
3. Choose OK or press ⏎Enter.

Exercise 1.1: Using the Window Zoom Command

For the exercises in this chapter, open the financial worksheet (C5LP2.XLS) you saved in the second long project at the end of Chapter 5.

In this exercise, you use the Window Zoom command to see more of the worksheet.

1. Open the Window menu, and choose the Zoom command. The Zoom dialog box appears (see fig. 7.1).

2. Select the 50% Zoom option.

3. Choose OK or press ⏎Enter.

4. Return to the standard Zoom size by opening the Window menu and choosing the Zoom command. Select the 100% option. Choose OK or press ⏎Enter.

Exercise 1.2: Using the Window Zoom Command

In this exercise, you increase the magnification of an area on the C5LP2.XLS worksheet.

1. Make cell A8 the active cell.

2. Open the Window menu, and choose the Zoom command. The Zoom dialog box appears (see fig. 7.1).

3. Select the 200% Zoom option.

4. Choose OK or press ⏎Enter.

5. Return to the standard Zoom size by opening the Window menu and choosing the Zoom command. Select the 100% option. Choose OK or press ⏎Enter.

Objective 2: To Set Up the Page

Sometimes you may want to change certain printer settings for a single document only. Excel's File Page Setup command enables you to change printer settings that affect only the active document. When you choose the File Page Setup command, the Page Setup dialog box appears (see fig. 7.2). You use the options in this dialog box to control the way the document appears on the page.

The File Page Setup command enables you to modify certain default printer settings and affect the active document only. The File Page Setup command also provides capabilities for adding headers and footers to a document, changing margins, turning on or off worksheet gridlines, choosing page order, and positioning spreadsheet data on the page. Table 7.2 outlines the options that the File Page Setup command provides in the Page Setup dialog box.

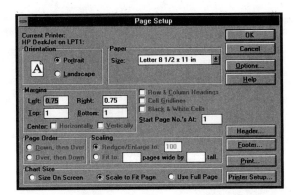

Fig. 7.2
The Page Setup
dialog box.

Table 7.2 Page Setup Options	
Option	*Description*
Orientation	Portrait option prints worksheet columns vertically down the length of the paper. Landscape prints rows vertically down the length of the paper. Landscape is used when you have few rows but many columns of data in your worksheet and need to fit all the columns on one page.
Paper	Specifies Size of paper, including letter, legal, executive, or envelope (A4)
Margins	Controls amount of space between Left, Right, Top, and Bottom edges of the paper and the printed document
Center	Centers the document Horizontally between left and right margins or Vertically between top and bottom margins
Page Order	Changes the page sequence on your worksheet. Down, then Over prints down page by page, then returns to top and prints down page by page.

continues

167

Table 7.2 Continued	
Option	*Description*
	Over, then Down prints across until all data is printed page by page, then goes down and prints across.
Scaling	Scales the area you want to print. Reduce/Enlarge to ___% magnifies or reduces the print area according to your specifications.
	Fit to ___ pages wide by ___ tall forces the reduction or enlargement of the print area to fill a specified number of pages.
Row & Column Headings	Turns row and column headings on or off for printing
Cell Gridlines	Turns worksheet gridlines on or off for printing
Black & White Cells	If color formats were used in cells and text boxes, they are removed when printing to a noncolor printer.
Start Page No.'s At	If page numbering is added in the header or footer, this option controls the starting page number.
Chart Size	Sizes chart according to screen size, to page size, or to full page size, adjusting height-to-width ratio. This option appears only when printing charts.
Options Button	Tunnels directly into the Printer Setup/Options dialog box
Header Button	Brings up dialog box that enables you to specify text, page numbering, date, time, and file name to be printed at the top of each page

7

Option	Description
Footer Button	Brings up dialog box that enables you to specify text, page numbering, date, time, and file name to be printed at the bottom of each page
Print Button	Displays the Print dialog box
Printer Setup Button	Displays the Printer Setup dialog box and enables you to change to another defined printer or change default printer settings

Exercise 2.1: Using the Page Setup Command To Change Settings

7

In this exercise, you change the default page print settings in the C5LP2.XLS worksheet.

1. Print the C5LP2.XLS worksheet. The worksheet will print according to the default page setup settings.
2. Open the File menu, and choose the Page Setup command. The Page Setup dialog box appears (see fig. 7.2).
3. Select the Landscape option in the Orientation section of the Page Setup dialog box.
4. Select the Row & Column Headings option.
5. Click the Cell Gridlines check box to turn off this setting. (The X should disappear.)
6. Choose the Print button to print the worksheet with the new Page Setup settings.

Exercise 2.2: Using the Page Setup Command To Return to the Default Settings

In this exercise, you return to the default settings in the C5LP2.XLS worksheet.

1. Open the File menu, and choose the Page Setup command. The Page Setup dialog box appears (see fig. 7.2).

2. Select the Portrait option in the Orientation section of the Page Setup dialog box.

3. Click the Row & Column Headings check box to turn off this setting. (The X should disappear.)

4. Select the Cell Gridlines option.

5. Choose the Print button to print the worksheet with these Page Setup settings.

Creating Headers and Footers

A header or footer creates a consistent look across all the pages of a document. You can use a header, for example, to place a title at the top of each page. And you can use a footer to automatically number each page at the bottom. Headers and footers appear .50" from the top or bottom of the paper and .75" from the left or right edge of the paper. A header or footer can include items such as text, a page number, the current date and time, and formatting such as bold and italics.

The Header and Footer dialog boxes have three sections in which to include information that will print on each page (see fig. 7.3). The left section inserts text aligned with the left margin; the center section inserts information centered on the page; and the right section inserts information aligned with the right margin.

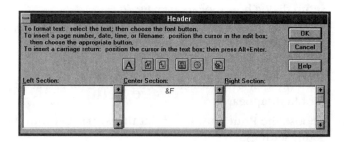

Fig. 7.3
The Header
dialog box.

When you select one of these three sections and choose the appropriate icon, Excel will include the information specified at the top or bottom of each page and aligned as you indicate. By selecting the information you want to include as a header or footer and choosing the Format Font icon (the boxed A) in the Header or Footer dialog box, you can format the header or footer in various fonts.

Excel uses codes to assign formatting. When you click the icons in the Header or Footer dialog box, a code is inserted into the appropriate section. All codes begin with an ampersand (&) and are followed by a letter. The default header setting is a &F, which prints the file name centered at the top of the page. The default footer setting is Page &P, which prints the word *Page* followed by the page number centered at the bottom of the page. Table 7.3 lists the other header and footer icons you use to insert codes.

Table 7.3 Header and Footer Icons	
Icon	*Description*
A	Enables you to choose a font for selected header or footer text
	Inserts page number
	Indicates the total number of pages in document
	Inserts date
	Inserts time
	Inserts file name

Exercise 2.3: Using the Page Setup Command To Print Headers

In this exercise, you print your name in the left side of the header in the C5LP2.XLS worksheet.

1. Open the File menu, and choose the Page Setup command. The Page Setup dialog box appears (see fig. 7.2).
2. Click the Header button. The Header dialog box appears (see fig. 7.3).
3. Type your name; it will appear in the Left Section window.
4. Choose OK to close the Header dialog box.
5. Choose OK to close the Page Setup dialog box.
6. Print the worksheet, and you will see the header.

7

Exercise 2.4: Using the Page Setup Command To Print Footers

In this exercise, you print a message in the right side of the footer in the C5LP2.XLS worksheet.

1. Open the File menu, and choose the Page Setup command. The Page Setup dialog box appears (see fig. 7.2).

2. Click the Footer button. The Footer dialog box appears.

3. Click in the Right Section window. Type MY WORKSHEET.

4. Choose OK to close the Footer dialog box.

5. Choose OK to close the Page Setup dialog box.

6. Print the worksheet, and you will see the footer.

Defining the Print Area

To print a portion of a worksheet, you must define that portion as a print area. If you select nonadjoining sections of your worksheet and define the multiple sections as a single print area, Excel prints each nonadjoining area on a separate page. If you do not define a print area, Excel assumes that you want to define the entire worksheet as the print area.

To define a print area, follow these steps:

1. Select the range you want to print. To select multiple nonadjoining ranges using the mouse, hold down Ctrl as you select the ranges. Excel prints each range on a separate page.

2. Open the Options menu, and choose the Set Print Area command. This command names the selection Print_Area. The area is surrounded by a dashed border that indicates the area you will print.

Exercise 2.5: Defining a Print Area

In this exercise, you define a print area in the C5LP2.XLS worksheet.

1. Select the cells A5 through B17 as the range you want to print.

2. Open the Options menu, and choose the Set Print Area command. This command names the selection Print_Area. The area is surrounded by a dashed border that indicates the area you will print.

3. Print the worksheet. Only the range you defined as the print area will print.

7

172

Exercise 2.6: Removing a Print Area

In this exercise, you remove the print area you have set in the C5LP2.XLS worksheet.

1. Click the Select All button on the worksheet. This button is located above the row 1 heading and to the left of the column A heading. Clicking this button selects the whole worksheet. Or, if you prefer to use the keyboard, press `Ctrl`+`⇧Shift`+space bar.

2. Open the Options menu, and choose the Remove Print Area command.

3. Print the worksheet. The entire worksheet will print.

Inserting Page Breaks

If you select an area for printing that cannot fit on a single page, Excel inserts automatic page breaks. A page break appears as a dashed line between the end of one page and the beginning of the next page. If you are not satisfied with the location of the automatic page break, you have the option of inserting manual page breaks. A manual page break enables you to control where a page ends. After you insert a manual page break, the automatic page break readjusts downward to affect pages below. To insert a page break, select the cell below and to the right of the location where you want the page to break. Choose the Options Set Page Break command. A manual page break appears above and to the left of the active cell. Manual page breaks appear on-screen as bold dashed lines.

To insert a horizontal page break only, select the entire row below where you want to insert the page break. (Click the row number to select the entire row.) Choose the Options Set Page Break command. To insert a vertical page break only, select the entire column to the left of where you want to insert the page break. (Click the column letter to select the entire column.) Choose the Options Set Page Break command. In fig. 7.4, a manual horizontal page break was inserted above the Expenses section.

You can delete a manual page break by selecting the cell below and to the right of the page break intersection. If the correct cell is selected, the Options menu displays the Remove Page Break command rather than the Set Page Break command. An automatic page break cannot be removed.

7

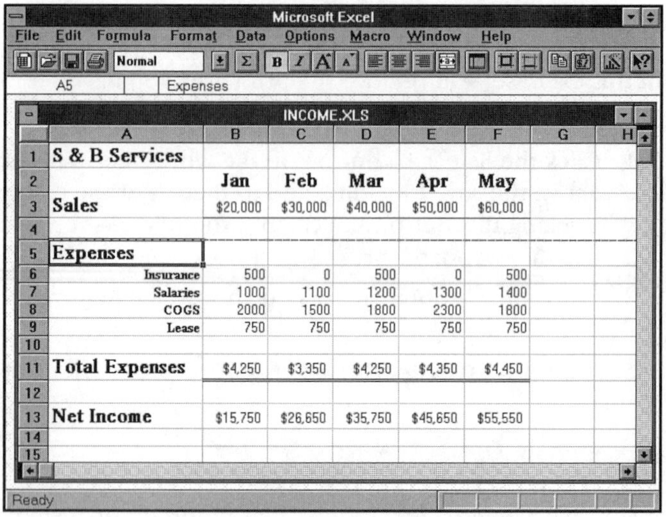

Fig. 7.4
A manual page
break.

Exercise 2.7: Inserting a Horizontal Page Break

In this exercise, you insert a horizontal page break only between rows 12 and 13 in the C5LP2.XLS worksheet.

1. Select the entire row below where you want to insert the page break. (Click the row number 13 to select the entire row.)

2. Open the Options menu, and choose the Set Page Break command.

3. To remove the horizontal page break, select the entire row below where you inserted the page break. (Click the row number 13 to select the entire row.) Choose the Options Remove Page Break command.

Exercise 2.8: Inserting a Vertical Page Break

In this exercise, you insert a vertical page break only between columns B and C in the C5LP2.XLS worksheet.

1. Select the entire column to the right of where you want to insert the page break. (Click the column C heading to select the entire column.)

2. Open the Options menu, and choose the Set Page Break command.

3. To remove the vertical page break, select the entire column to the right of where you inserted the page break. (Click the column C heading.) Choose the Options Remove Page Break command.

174

You can remove all manual page breaks in a worksheet after the entire worksheet is selected. To do so, follow these steps:

1. Select the entire worksheet by clicking the Select All button on the worksheet. This button is located above the row 1 heading and to the left of the column A heading. Or press Ctrl + ⇧Shift + space bar. The entire worksheet is selected.

2. Open the Options menu, and choose the Remove Page Break command. All manual page breaks disappear.

Objective 3: To Preview a Document

Because a worksheet is actually one large grid of cells, you may have difficulty visualizing what a document will look like when you print it. Excel's **File Print Preview** command enables you to view your document before you print it. In Preview mode, you have a bird's-eye view of what the document will look like on the page. The preview feature also includes options that enable you to change the margins of the document, change column width, and zoom in on a section of the document to view a section up close.

After you have defined a print area with the **Options Set Print Area** command, you can view the area by choosing the **File Print Preview** command. Remember: Defining a print area is necessary only if you choose to print selected areas of the entire worksheet. You can print the document by clicking the **Print** button at the top of the Preview window (see fig. 7.5.).

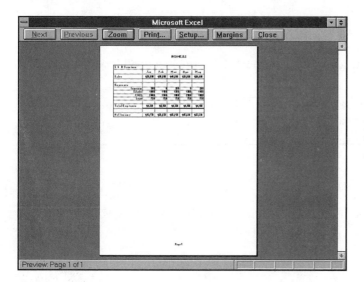

Fig. 7.5
The Preview window.

Scrolling

The buttons across the top of the Preview window include **Next** and **Previous**. You can use these buttons for moving from one page to the next in Preview mode. If you are previewing a document that is a single page, the **Next** and **Previous** buttons are dimmed. If you are previewing multiple pages, the **Next** button is available only if a page follows the page you are viewing. The **Previous** button is available only if a page precedes the page you are viewing.

Zooming

In Preview mode, you may not be able to see the exact detail of your document. If you need a close-up view of the document, you can zoom in and view enlarged sections of it.

To use the Zoom feature in a document, follow these steps:

1. Position the mouse pointer over the section you want to see enlarged and click once. (The mouse pointer changes to a magnifying glass when positioned over any part of the document.)
2. Use the vertical and horizontal scroll bars to move to other sections while maintaining the enlarged view.
3. Click the left mouse button once to zoom out and see the entire page.
4. Choose the Close button to exit Preview mode and return to the active document.

Exercise 3.1: Previewing Your Worksheet

In this exercise, you see what the C5LP2.XLS worksheet will look like before you print.

1. Open the File menu, and choose the Print Preview command. The document appears in the Preview window.
2. Remain in Preview for the next exercise.

Exercise 3.2: Zooming in the Preview mode

In this exercise, you use the Zoom feature on the C5LP2.XLS worksheet in Preview mode. If you have not already done so, complete Exercise 3.1 before starting this exercise.

1. Position the mouse pointer over the section you want to see enlarged and click once. (The mouse pointer changes to a magnifying glass when positioned over any part of the document.)

2. Use the vertical and horizontal scroll bars to move to other sections while maintaining the enlarged view.

3. Click the left mouse button once to zoom out and see the entire page.

4. Choose the Close button to exit Preview mode and return to the active document.

Objective 4: To Print a Document

After setting up the printer and document, you are ready to execute the **File Print** command. This command controls the number of copies you print, the number of pages, and the quality of the printing. The Print dialog box is set up to print one copy of all pages of the worksheet or macro sheet unless you select other options (see fig. 7.6). The Print options are described in table 7.4.

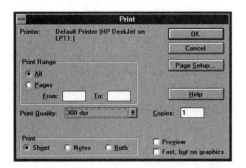

Fig. 7.6
The Print dialog box.

Table 7.4 Print Options	
Option	*Description*
All	Print Range option that enables you to print the entire worksheet (or defined print area)
Pages	Print Range option that enables you to specify certain pages to print

continues

177

Table 7.4 Continued	
Option	*Description*
From and To	Text boxes that enable you to define the first page you want to print (From) through the last page (To). You must select the Pages option to use these text boxes.
Print Quality	Displays resolution levels available on currently selected printer
Copies	Specifies number of copies to print
Print	Sheet prints only the active worksheet; Notes prints only cell notes you have created; Both prints both the worksheet and cell notes on separate pages.
Preview	Displays document in Print Preview window when you choose OK
Fast, but no graphics	Prints document without graphics
Page Setup Button	Displays the Page Setup dialog box

To complete the printing process, follow these steps:

1. Open the File menu, and choose the Print command. The Print dialog box appears (see fig. 7.6).

2. To preview the document you are about to print, select the Preview check box to turn on this option.

3. Select the options you want, or accept the default settings.

4. Choose OK or press ⏎Enter. If you did not select the Preview check box, printing begins. If you selected the Preview check box, you enter Preview mode. You can execute the Print command in Preview mode.

To print quickly, use the Print tool on the Standard Toolbar. The Print tool immediately executes printing, without displaying the Print dialog box.

Exercise 4.1: Printing Multiple Copies of Your Document

In this exercise, you print three copies of the C5LP2.XLS worksheet.

1. Make sure that the C5LP2.XLS worksheet is open.
2. Open the File menu, and choose the Print command. The Print dialog box appears (see fig. 7.6).
3. Click in the Copies text box, and change the number in the box to 3.
4. To print, choose OK or press ⏎Enter.

Summary

This chapter introduced you to many aspects of viewing and printing in Excel. You learned how to view an enlarged or reduced view of your document; using the Zoom features; how to control the way a page is set up before you print; and how to insert and remove manual page breaks, define print areas, and add headers and footers to a document. You also learned about Print Preview and the options included in Preview mode for zooming.

The following chapter will introduce you to charting, which is one of Excel's most exciting and powerful features. In Chapter 8, "Charting Data," you will learn how to create a chart as a separate document and how to create a chart on a worksheet. You also will learn how to change to another chart type, format a chart, and print a chart.

Testing Your Knowledge

True/False Questions

1. Using the Window Zoom command changes the way a worksheet will print.
2. The default footer code setting in Excel is $F.
3. Before you can print a portion of a worksheet, you must first define that portion as a print area.
4. A page break in your worksheet appears on-screen as a solid double line.
5. Manual page breaks cannot be removed.

Multiple Choice Questions

1. The Print command is found on the _____ menu.
   A. Window
   B. Output
   C. Options
   D. File

2. Excel creates automatic _____ if the area you want to print will not print on one page.
   A. text boxes
   B. page breaks
   C. formatting changes
   D. views

3. The _____ command enables you to specify the number of copies you print.
   A. Options Output
   B. Worksheet Copies
   C. File Print
   D. none of these answers

4. If you cannot print all the columns in your worksheet on one page, then you should select _____ orientation.
   A. Landscape
   B. Portrait
   C. wrap
   D. 50% Zoom

5. Automatic page breaks cannot be _____
   A. seen on-screen.
   B. removed.
   C. defaulted.
   D. none of these answers

Fill-in-the-Blank Questions

1. You can change the margins of your worksheet when it prints by using the File _____ command.
2. A _____ is information that prints in the top margin of a worksheet printout.
3. _____ numbers are displayed in the footer of a worksheet printout.
4. To see what a worksheet will look like before you print it, you can use the _____ command.
5. To specify different print settings and display options for separate areas of a worksheet, you use the Window _____ command.

Review: Short Projects

1. Printing a Worksheet with Modified Print Settings

   Open the NSCC COMPANY QUARTERLY REPORT worksheet (C4LP1.XLS) that you built in the first long project at the end of Chapter 4. Print two copies without gridlines; print one copy without gridlines and with the column letters and row numbers on the printout.

2. Printing a Worksheet with Manual Page Breaks

   Print the NSCC COMPANY QUARTERLY REPORT worksheet (C4LP1.XLS) with a vertical page break between columns C and D. Remove the vertical page break, and print the worksheet with a page break between the TOTAL EXPENSES row and the SALES row. Then remove the horizontal page break.

3. Exploring the Window Zoom Command

   Use the various preset magnifications and reductions available with the Window Zoom command.

Review: Long Projects

1. Printing a Wide Worksheet

   Open the NSCC COMPANY QUARTERLY REPORT worksheet (C4LP1.XLS) that you built in the first long project at the end of Chapter 4. Expand the column widths of columns B, C, D, E, and F to a width of 18. Preview the printout of the worksheet, and then print it. Try to delete the automatic page breaks Excel inserts—but don't try too long! Change the print orientation to Landscape. Preview the printout, and then print the worksheet.

2. Printing a Worksheet with Headers and Footers

Open the NSCC COMPANY QUARTERLY REPORT worksheet (C4LP1.XLS) that you built in the first long project at the end of Chapter 4. Create headers and footers that contain information you want printed on the printout. Then print the worksheet with these headers and footers. Delete the headers and footers, and print the worksheet again.

7

Charting Data

Data can be interpreted much faster if it is represented in a graphical format. A chart provides a graphical format that has a greater visual impact than rows of numbers in a worksheet. A chart can communicate results that are recognized at a glance.

Charting data in an Excel worksheet is a simple process. Excel offers three ways to create a chart. You can create a chart as a separate document using the **File New Chart** menu command. You can create an embedded chart on a worksheet using Excel's ChartWizard, which guides you step-by-step through the process. Or you can use the Chart Toolbar to quickly create an embedded chart on a worksheet.

Excel offers many features you can use to enhance and edit a chart. You can choose from among many chart types including column, bar, area, line, pie, scatter, radar, and surface charts. Excel offers six three-dimensional chart types. Each chart type includes several predefined charts you can select from the Chart Toolbar or the Chart Gallery.

This chapter covers the steps involved in creating a chart; selecting a chart type; and enhancing, formatting, modifying, and printing a chart.

Objectives

1. To Create a Chart
2. To Enhance and Format a Chart
3. To Print a Chart

Key Terms in This Chapter	
X-axis	The horizontal (category) axis on a chart
Y-axis	The vertical (value) axis on a chart
Chart tool	The Excel tool used to create a chart on a worksheet
Attached text	Text on a chart (such as the chart title) that is fixed to a position and cannot be moved
Chart object	An item on a chart (such as an arrow) that can be moved, sized, and formatted
Patterns dialog box	The dialog box that appears when you double-click a chart object; enables you to choose a border format, as well as patterns for the area inside the border for most chart objects
Legend	A guide displayed near the chart that identifies the data in the chart
Data series	A collection of data from a worksheet
ChartWizard	A charting tool used to guide you step-by-step through the process of creating and formatting a chart

8

Objective 1: To Create a Chart

Charts are based on selected data in a worksheet. After data is selected on a worksheet, creating a chart is as simple as pressing a single key. Excel displays the selected data in a column chart, which is the default chart type. Excel automatically decides how to plot the chart and how to set up the X- and Y-axis. Excel plots the chart based on the size of the numbers in the worksheet and the layout of the selected worksheet data. Later in this chapter, you will learn how to change the default chart type and layout, and to enhance your chart with formatting.

To create a chart as a separate document, follow these steps:

1. Select the worksheet data you want to chart. If you are unsure of how to select data, refer to Chapter 3, "Excel Worksheet Basics," for more detailed instructions.

2. Open the File menu, and choose the New command. The New dialog box appears.

3. Select Chart from the dialog box, and choose OK or press ⏎Enter. The selected range of data is charted in a separate window.

The chart is linked to the selected worksheet data. If the data changes, the chart adjusts to reflect the change.

Exercise 1.1: Creating a Chart Using the File New Chart Command

The exercises in this chapter use the QTRSALES.XLS worksheet in fig. 8.1. Enter the QTRSALES.XLS worksheet as it is shown, and save it in a file on your disk. You will use this worksheet in all the exercises in this chapter. Because the exercises build on each other, complete the exercises in order. If you cannot complete all the exercises in one session, be sure to save your work before exiting Excel.

To create a chart from the QTRSALES.XLS worksheet using the File New Chart command, follow these steps:

1. Select the range of cells from A4 to D8 (see fig. 8.1).

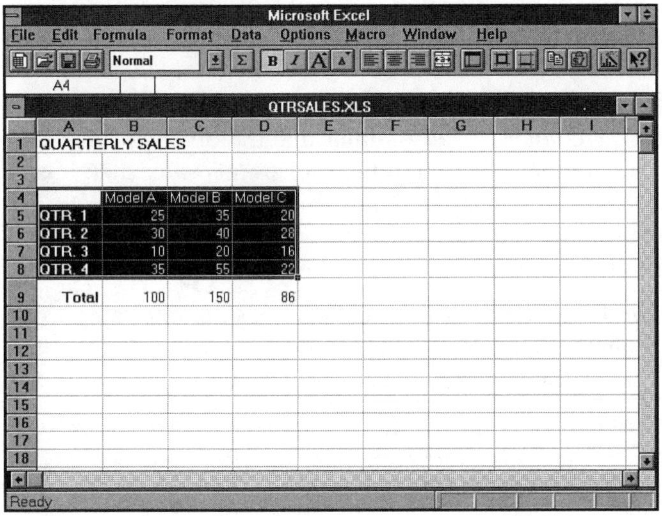

8

Fig. 8.1
The
QTRSALES.XLS
worksheet.

2. Open the File menu, and choose the New command. The New dialog box appears.

3. Select Chart from the dialog box.

4. Choose OK or press ↵Enter. The selected range of data is charted in a separate window (see fig. 8.2).

5. To display both the chart and the worksheet, choose the Window Arrange Vertical command.

Fig. 8.2
The chart for the selected data.

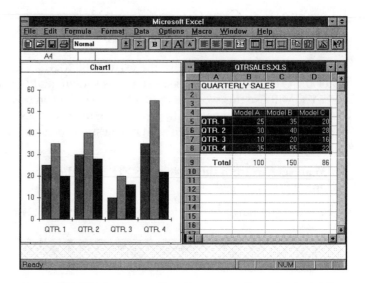

8

When Excel charts the selected data, Excel assumes that the category (X) axis runs along the longest side of the selection. If the selection is taller than it is wide, the category labels are taken from the leftmost column in the selection (see fig. 8.2). If the selection is wider than it is tall, the category labels are taken from the first row of the selection.

If the selection is equal in length and width, Excel assumes that the category (X) labels are contained in the first row of the selection. Later in this chapter, you will learn how to change these default chart orientations.

If Excel is not sure how to lay out and plot the selected data, a dialog box appears on-screen and requests more information about plotting data (see fig. 8.3). For example, if every selected cell contains a value, Excel will prompt you to specify what the first column of selected data contains: First Data Series, Category (X) Axis Labels, or X-Values for an XY-Chart.

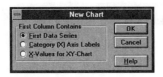

Fig. 8.3
The New Chart
dialog box.

Choose one of the options: **First Data Series**, **Category (X) Axis Labels**, or **X-Values for XY Chart**. Choose OK or press `⏎Enter` to clear the dialog box and proceed with plotting the selected data.

The chart appears in a separate window with its own menu bar. The commands on the menu bar apply to the chart. For example, the chart menu bar includes the **Chart** and **Gallery** menus, which are not included on the worksheet menu bar. The Format menu on the chart menu bar is different from the Format menu on the worksheet menu bar. The Format menu on the chart menu bar contains formatting commands that pertain to charts. The chart commands are outlined in table 8.1.

Table 8.1 Chart Commands	
Command	*Action*
Gallery Preferred	Applies the format you defined with the **Gallery Set Preferred** command
Gallery Set Preferred	Changes the default chart format to one that you specify
Chart Attach Text	Inserts text in a fixed location on the chart, such as along the X- or Y-axis
Chart Add Arrow	Adds (or deletes) an arrow on a chart
Chart Add Legend	Adds (or deletes) a legend on a chart
Chart Axes	Hides or displays the category (X) and value (Y) axes
Chart Gridlines	Displays or hides major and minor gridlines attached to the category and value axes
Chart Add Overlay	Adds (or deletes) a second chart over the current main chart to create a combination chart
Chart Edit Series	Creates, edits, or deletes a data series on an active chart

continues

8

187

Table 8.1 Continued	
Command	*Action*
Chart Select Chart	Selects all elements of a chart, enabling Edit commands to affect all aspects of the chart
Chart Select Plot Area	Selects a chart's plot area, enabling the Format Patterns command to affect all elements in the area bounded by the axes
Chart Protect (Unprotect)	Protects (or unprotects) a chart's data series, formatting, and document window from change; provides password protection
Chart Color Palette	Customizes colors in the Color Palette and copies Color Palettes between open documents
Chart Calculate Now	Recalculates all open worksheets, and then redraws all open charts supported by those worksheets when manual calculation is on
Chart Spelling	Checks the spelling of text, unusual capitalization, and repeated words in the active chart window
Format Patterns	Sets the style, weight, color, and pattern of selected chart object
Format Font	Changes the font for selected chart text
Format Text	Sets the alignment and orientation of text in a chart
Format Scale	Controls the scale setting for each axis on the active chart
Format Legend	Changes the position of the chart's legend
Format Main Chart	Sets the active main chart's type and formatting; enables you to change chart types without losing custom formatting
Format Overlay	Sets the active overlay chart's type and formatting
Format 3-D View	Controls the angle at which you view the data in a 3-D chart

8

Command	Action
Format Move	Enables you to move selected chart objects
Format Size	Enables you to resize chart arrows and unattached text boxes in a chart

In addition to displaying a different menu bar, a chart window also displays the Chart Toolbar (see fig. 8.4). The Chart Toolbar contains tools for changing to another chart type and chart formatting tools.

Most of the tools on the Chart Toolbar represent chart types. There are 17 Chart Type tools on the Toolbar. The Toolbar also includes the ChartWizard tool, plus tools for enhancing a chart with gridlines, legends, arrows, and text.

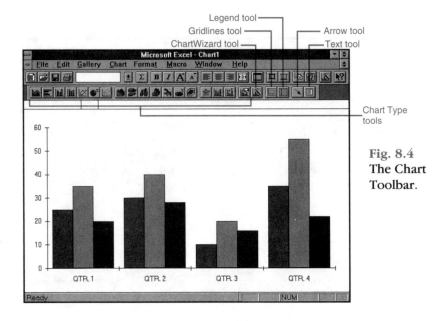

Fig. 8.4
The Chart
Toolbar.

Creating an Embedded Chart on a Worksheet

In the previous section, you learned how to create a chart as a separate document from the worksheet document. In many cases, you will want the worksheet data and chart on separate pages. Sometimes, however, you will want to have your worksheet data and the chart that represents the data on the same page. You can use the Chart Toolbar or the ChartWizard tool on the Standard Toolbar to plot selected data on a worksheet.

Using the ChartWizard

The ChartWizard tool will guide you with a series of dialog boxes through the process of creating a chart. The ChartWizard is a five-step method that automatically charts selected data and prompts you to select a chart type and a chart format, edit the way the data is plotted, and add gridlines, a legend, and a title. At each step, the ChartWizard window displays a sample of the chart as it will appear with your choices. When the ChartWizard is completed, the chart becomes a graphic object embedded on the worksheet.

Step 1 of the ChartWizard displays the range of selected data to chart (see fig. 8.5). Step 2 of the ChartWizard prompts you to select the type of chart you want (see fig. 8.6).

Fig. 8.5
Step 1: Displaying the range of data.

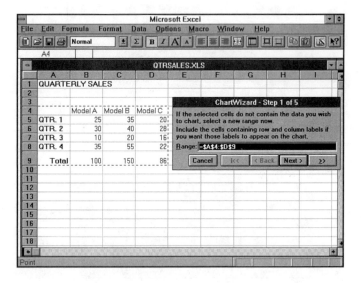

Step 3 of the ChartWizard prompts you to select from among the predefined formats available for the chart type you selected in step 2 (see fig. 8.7). Step 4 of the ChartWizard enables you to edit the way the data is plotted (see fig. 8.8).

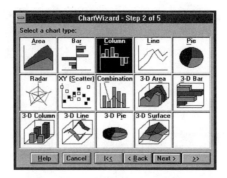

Fig. 8.6
Step 2: Selecting a
chart type.

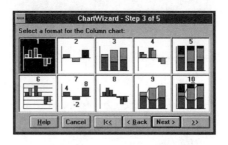

Fig. 8.7
Step 3: Selecting
predefined chart
formats.

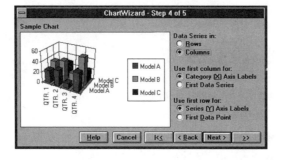

Fig. 8.8
Step 4: Selecting
how to plot
the data.

8

The final step of the ChartWizard prompts you to apply formatting, such as
adding gridlines to the background of the plot area, adding a legend, and
adding titles (see fig. 8.9).

Each ChartWizard window contains buttons you can use to move around the
ChartWizard. Table 8.2 lists the function of each ChartWizard button.

Fig. 8.9
Step 5: Selecting
formatting.

Button	Function
Next	Move to the next ChartWizard step
Back	Return to the previous ChartWizard step
>>	Create the chart displayed in the ChartWizard sample area and exit the ChartWizard
<<	Return to step 1 of the ChartWizard
Cancel	Stop the ChartWizard and return to your worksheet without creating a chart
Help	Get instructions about ChartWizard options

Table 8.2 ChartWizard Buttons

To create an embedded chart on a worksheet using the ChartWizard, follow these steps:

1. Select the data you want to chart.

2. Click the ChartWizard tool on the Standard Toolbar.

3. Position the mouse pointer on the worksheet area in the upper left corner where you want the chart to start. The mouse pointer changes to a cross hair when positioned in the worksheet area.

   Drag diagonally toward the lower right corner until the border defines the area you want the chart to occupy. Release the mouse button (see fig. 8.10).

   Note: If you want to plot the chart in a perfect square, hold down ⇧Shift while you drag the mouse. If you want to align the chart with the worksheet gridlines, hold down Ctrl while you drag the mouse.

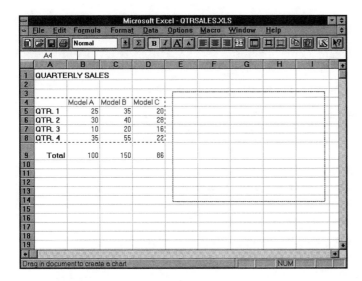

Fig. 8.10
Defining the chart
area.

The first dialog box appears with the selected range defined in the
Range box.

4. Choose the **N**ext button to continue through the five steps of the
   ChartWizard.

5. Choose OK or press ⏎Enter when you reach the Step 5 of 5
   ChartWizard dialog box.

The chart in the ChartWizard sample area is embedded in the area of your
worksheet defined in step 3 of these instructions (see fig. 8.11).

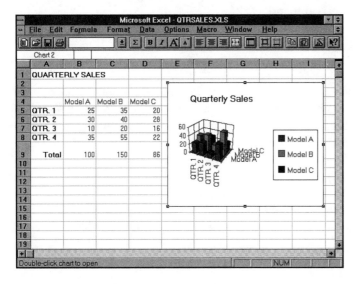

Fig. 8.11
The embedded
chart.

Exercise 1.2: Creating a Chart Using the ChartWizard

In this exercise, you create a chart from the QTRSALES.XLS worksheet using the ChartWizard.

1. Select the range of cells from A4 to D8.
2. Click the ChartWizard tool on the Standard Toolbar.
3. Drag the mouse pointer over cells A11 to F17 to define the location for the embedded chart. Release the mouse button. The Step 1 of 5 ChartWizard dialog box appears.
4. Choose the Next button in the Step 1, Step 2, Step 3, and Step 4 windows.
5. Choose OK or press ⏎Enter in the Step 5 window.

At some point, you probably will have to edit the embedded chart using charting commands that are only available in a chart window. For example, if you are working with a 3-D chart, you may decide you want to rotate the chart to a particular view. Rotating a 3-D chart can only be accomplished in a chart window. To display an embedded chart in a chart window, position the mouse on the chart and double-click the left mouse button. The embedded chart appears in a chart window.

Any changes you make to the chart in the chart window will automatically appear in the embedded chart on the worksheet. When you have completed editing the chart in the chart window, choose the Window menu and select the worksheet containing the embedded chart.

If you want to save an embedded chart in a separate file, double-click the chart and use the File Save As command.

Using the Chart Toolbar

The previous section covered creating an embedded chart using Excel's ChartWizard. You also can embed a chart in a worksheet using the Chart Toolbar. To create an embedded chart with this method, you must display the Chart Toolbar. This Toolbar appears at the bottom of the screen. If the Chart Toolbar is not displayed on-screen, follow these steps:

1. Open the Options menu, and choose the Toolbars command. The Toolbars dialog box appears (see fig. 8.12).

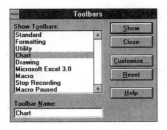

Fig. 8.12
The Toolbars
dialog box.

2. Select Chart from the Show Toolbars list box, and choose the Show button.

   Or position the mouse pointer on a blank area of the Standard Toolbar, and click the right mouse button. Choose Chart from the drop-down menu.

   The Chart Toolbar appears below the Standard Toolbar.

To create an embedded chart using the Chart Toolbar, follow these steps:

1. Select the data you want to chart.

2. Choose the chart type you want to create from the Chart Toolbar.

3. Position the mouse pointer on the worksheet area in the upper left corner where you want the chart to start. The mouse pointer changes to a cross hair when positioned in the worksheet area. Drag diagonally toward the lower right corner until the border defines the area you want the chart to occupy. Release the mouse button. A chart of the selected data appears in the worksheet area.

If you want to plot the chart in a perfect square, hold down ⌈⇧Shift⌉ while you drag the mouse. If you want to align the chart with the worksheet gridlines, hold down ⌈Ctrl⌉ while you drag the mouse.

If you want to change to another chart type, select the embedded chart and choose a Chart Type tool from the Toolbar.

If you are not sure what action a Chart tool performs, the status bar in the lower left corner of the Excel window displays a description of the selected tool when you click the tool and hold down the mouse button.

Exercise 1.3: Creating a Chart Using the Chart Toolbar

In this exercise, you create a chart from the QTRSALES.XLS worksheet using the Chart Toolbar.

1. Select the range of cells from A4 to D8.
2. Click the 3-D Pie Chart tool in the middle of the Chart Toolbar.
3. Drag the mouse pointer over cells A11 to F17 to define the location for the chart. Release the mouse button. The chart appears.

To display an embedded chart in a chart window, position the mouse pointer on the chart and double-click the left mouse button. The embedded chart appears in a chart window. Any changes you make to the chart in the chart window will automatically appear in the embedded chart on the worksheet. When you have completed editing the chart in a chart window, choose the Window menu and select the worksheet containing the embedded chart from the pull-down menu.

Moving a Chart

When you create a chart on a worksheet, the position and size may not suit you. If you want to make changes, you can move and resize the chart.

To move a chart on a worksheet, follow these steps:

1. Select the chart by clicking it. The chart is enclosed by boundary lines with small black handles.
2. Position the mouse pointer inside the chart area. Click the left mouse button, and drag the chart to the desired location (see fig. 8.13).

8

Fig. 8.13
Dragging the
selected chart.

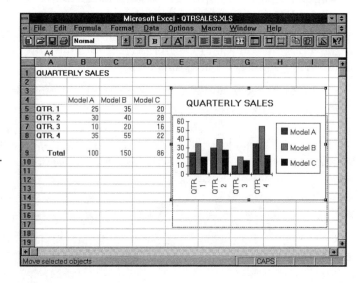

Sizing a Chart

When an embedded chart is selected on a worksheet, the chart appears enclosed by boundary lines with eight small black squares called *handles*. The black squares are used for sizing the area. The corner handles are used to size the chart proportionally. The handles in the middle between the corner handles are used to increase or decrease the chart horizontally or vertically. Changing the chart size will often change the display of the labels on the X-axis and the scaling of the Y-axis.

To resize the chart, follow these steps:

1. Select the chart.
2. Position the mouse pointer on one of the small black handles. The mouse pointer changes to a double-headed arrow when properly positioned on the handle.
3. Drag the handle until the chart reaches the desired size. The corner handles size the chart proportionally. The middle handles size the chart horizontally or vertically.

Note: If labels on the X-axis are vertical or broken into two or more layers ("scrunched together"), expanding the horizontal size (width) of the chart will make the labels more readable.

8

Exercise 1.4: Moving and Sizing a Chart

The chart you created in the previous exercise still should be selected (the black handles should appear around the edge of the chart). If not, select the chart by clicking in it. In this exercise, you move the selected chart and change its size.

To move the selected chart, follow these steps:

1. Place the mouse pointer in the selected chart, and hold down the left mouse button.
2. Drag the chart so that the top edge is in row 3 of the worksheet. Release the mouse button.

To change the size of the selected chart, follow these steps:

1. Place the mouse pointer on the black handle in the middle of the lower edge of the selected chart. The mouse pointer becomes a double-headed arrow.
2. Hold down the left mouse button, and drag to row 16 of the worksheet. Release the mouse button.

197

Selecting a Chart Type

The first section of this chapter discussed charts that appear in windows separate from your worksheet. When you create a chart in a separate window, the **Gallery** and **Chart** menus appear in the menu bar at the top of the screen. You can make selections from these menus. A Chart Toolbar also appears on-screen when you create a chart in a separate window. The Chart Toolbar enables you to choose other chart types, and to enhance and format charts.

When you create an embedded chart on a worksheet, however, you will notice that the worksheet menu bar does not include the **Gallery** and **Chart** menus. If you want to change to another chart type, enhance the chart, or format the chart, you must display the worksheet chart in a separate chart window. To do this, position the mouse pointer on the chart and double-click. The chart appears in a chart window with the Chart menu bar and Toolbar. The changes you make to the chart in the chart window will appear on the embedded worksheet chart when you close the separate chart window.

Excel uses a column chart as its default chart type. If you want to change to another chart type after the chart is created, you can choose a chart type from the Toolbar, and the chart will instantly change to the selected type. (If you are not sure what type of chart is represented by the Chart Type tool, the status bar in the lower left corner of the Excel window displays a description of the selected tool.) You also can select a chart type from the Chart Gallery. The Chart Gallery is a collection of the various types of charts. Your choices include eight 2-D chart types and six 3-D chart types. Each chart type has several predefined chart formats.

To select a chart type from the gallery, follow these steps:

1. Open the **Gallery** menu, and choose the chart type you want on the menu. The menu contains these chart types: **Area**, **Bar**, **Column**, **Line**, **Pie**, **Radar**, **XY (Scatter)**, **Combination**, **3-D Area**, **3-D Bar**, **3-D Column**, **3-D Line**, **3-D Pie**, and **3-D Surface**.

   Predefined chart formats for the selected chart type appear in the Chart Gallery dialog box.

2. Choose the style you want by double-clicking the example. Or select the chart, and choose OK or press ⏎Enter. To view other chart types in the gallery, choose the **Next** or **Previous** button.

Exercise 1.5: Selecting a Chart Type for an Embedded Chart

In this exercise, you change the chart type used in Exercise 1.4 from a pie chart to a line chart.

1. Double-click inside the chart.

2. Open the Gallery menu, and choose the Line chart type. The Chart Gallery dialog box appears.

3. In the Chart Gallery dialog box, choose OK to select the first type of line chart.

   The line chart is displayed. Notice that the pie chart displayed only one column of worksheet data, but the line chart can show all three columns of data.

4. Close the separate chart window by double-clicking the application Control menu icon in the upper left corner of the chart window.

5. The embedded pie chart is now a line chart.

Setting the Preferred Chart Type

8

As mentioned earlier, the default chart type is a 2-D column chart. The column chart, therefore, is set as the preferred chart type. If you consistently use a chart type other than the column chart, you can change the preferred chart type to the style you use most frequently. For example, if you consistently use a line chart to chart data from a particular worksheet, you can change the column chart to a line chart, and set the line chart as the preferred chart type. After a chart is set as the preferred chart type, the preferred chart type appears each time you create a chart. The preferred chart also can include formatting and enhancements.

To set a preferred chart type, follow these steps:

1. From the chart window, choose the chart type you want using the Gallery menu. Select the predefined format you want.

2. Add any custom formatting or enhancements you want (such as adding Patterns, Chart Legend, Arrow, Gridlines, and so on).

3. Open the Gallery menu, and choose the Set Preferred command.

The preferred chart type applies to all charts created in the active document. If you change to a chart type other than the preferred chart type, you can return to the preferred chart type by selecting the **G**allery **P**referred command.

Charting Data Stored in Nonadjoining Areas of a Worksheet

The easiest kind of worksheet data to chart is data that is in a continuous block of rows and columns. You simply select the block, and Excel creates the chart. But what if you need to graph data that is in two or more nonadjoining ranges on a worksheet?

Suppose that you are using the QTRSALES.XLS worksheet and you want a pie chart of the quarterly sales of Model C. The labels for the pie slices are in column A. The Model C data in column D is separated from these labels by two columns of data that you don't want in the chart.

To create the chart, you first select the labels in column A with the mouse. Next, you select the data in column D by holding down Ctrl and then dragging the mouse. Then you can create the chart from the selected data.

Exercise 1.6: Selecting Nonadjacent Ranges To Chart

In this exercise, you select two separated sets of data to chart in the QTRSALES.XLS worksheet.

1. Make sure that the embedded line chart is selected. Clear the embedded line chart from the screen by choosing the Edit Clear command.
2. Make D1 the active cell. This step deselects the previously selected range of cells.
3. Select the first set of data. To do this, position the cell pointer in cell A5, hold down the left mouse button, and drag to cell A8. Release the mouse button.
4. Select the second set of data. To do this, position the cell pointer in cell D5, press and hold down Ctrl, and then press the left mouse button. Drag to cell D8, and then release the mouse button and the Ctrl key. You should see both blocks of data selected on-screen.
5. To display the nonadjoining data in the preferred chart type, choose the File New Chart command.

Changing the Excel Default Chart Orientation

Earlier in this chapter, you learned that Excel uses several rules to design the layout of your chart. If the data you select is taller than it is wide, the category

8

labels used to mark off the horizontal (X) axis are taken from the leftmost column in the worksheet. Otherwise, the category labels are taken from the first row of the selection.

If Excel does not know how to lay out your chart, it will ask you for help by displaying a dialog box. But what do you do if Excel has laid out the chart according to its rules, and you want to change Excel's default chart orientation?

You can change a chart orientation most easily when you create the chart using ChartWizard. In the fourth dialog box of the series displayed by ChartWizard, (Step 4 of 5), look at the Sample Chart window. If the data is not plotted the way you want to see it, follow these steps:

1. Click the unselected option button under Data Series in: (see fig. 8.8). You then see Excel's alternative chart in the Sample Chart window.

2. Choose the Next button to continue creating your chart.

Exercise 1.7: Changing the Excel Default Chart Orientation Using ChartWizard

8

In this exercise, you change the default chart orientation when creating a chart with the ChartWizard in the QTRSALES.XLS worksheet. Before you begin this exercise, clear any embedded chart by selecting the chart and choosing the Edit Clear command. Then select the range of cells from A4 to D8.

1. Click the ChartWizard tool, and then drag over cells A11 to F17. The Step 1 of 5 ChartWizard dialog box appears.

2. Choose the Next button in the Step 1, Step 2, and Step 3 dialog boxes.

   In the Sample Chart window of the Step 4 dialog box, you see the default chart plot.

3. Click the Rows option button under Data Series in:. The alternate chart appears in the Sample Chart window.

   You may find it instructive to click the Columns option button, study the default chart, and then click the Rows option button again so that the differences between the charts become clear to you.

4. Choose the Next button.

5. In the Step 5 dialog box, choose OK or press ⏎Enter.

To change the Excel default chart orientation when using the File New Chart command, follow these steps:

1. Select the worksheet data to chart, and copy it to the Clipboard by using the **Edit Copy** command.

2. Choose the **File New Chart** command. A new, empty chart window appears.

3. Choose the **Edit Paste Special** command. The Paste Special dialog box appears.

4. Click the unselected option button `Values (Y) in`.

5. Choose OK or press `⏎Enter`.

The chart that is the alternative to Excel's default is displayed in the chart window.

Exercise 1.8: Changing the Excel Default Chart Orientation When Using the File New Chart Command

In this exercise, you change the Excel default chart orientation when using the File New Chart command. Before starting this exercise, clear the embedded chart from your worksheet. Then follow these steps:

1. Select the range of cells from A4 to D8, and copy the range to the Clipboard by using the **Edit Copy** command.

2. Choose the **File New Chart** command. A new, empty chart window appears.

3. Choose the **Edit Paste Special** command. The Paste Special dialog box appears.

4. Click the **R**ows option button under `Values (Y) in`.

5. Choose OK or press `⏎Enter`.

The chart that is the alternative to Excel's default is displayed in the chart window.

Objective 2: To Enhance and Format a Chart

The Chart menu bar includes a number of commands you can use to enhance a chart. The chart commands enable you to add text, arrows, legends, and gridlines. You can format a chart object by double-clicking the object to access the Patterns dialog box, or by choosing commands from the Format menu. Fig. 8.14 shows the various components of an enhanced chart.

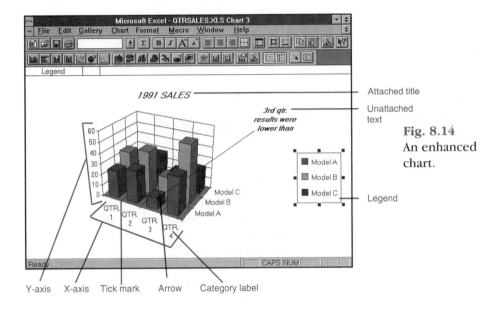

Fig. 8.14
An enhanced
chart.

Adding Text to a Chart

8

You can add text to a chart in the form of a chart title or a label attached to an axis or a data point. This type of text on a chart is referred to as *attached text*. You can attach text to the horizontal (X) axis, the vertical (Y) axis, and the chart title. Attached text is centered and fixed to the option selected, and cannot be moved. You also can include *unattached text* in an Excel chart. You can enter unattached text using the Text tool on the Chart Toolbar. The chart spell checker will check the spelling of all text in the chart. This section covers adding attached and unattached text.

Adding Attached Text

To attach text to a chart section, display the chart window and follow these steps:

1. Open the Chart menu, and choose the Attach Text command. The Attach Text dialog box appears (see fig. 8.15).

Fig. 8.15
The Attach Text
dialog box.

2. Select the type of text you want to add. The attached text options are described in table 8.3.

3. Choose OK or press ⏎Enter to clear the dialog box and attach text to the chart.

4. Edit the attached text in the formula bar as necessary.

Table 8.3	Attached Text Options
Option	*Function*
Chart Title	Centers a title in the plot area
Value (Y) Axis	Attaches a Y on the vertical Y-axis. This option changes to Value (Z) Axis for 3-D charts.
Category (X) Axis	Attaches an X on the horizontal X-axis
Series (Y) Axis	Attaches a Y on the vertical series axis of a 3-D chart
Series and Data Point	Attaches a number representing a data point
Overlay Value (Y) Axis	Attaches a Y on the overlay vertical axis
Overlay Category (X) Axis	Attaches an X on the overlay horizontal axis. (Overlay options are not available for 3-D charts.)

If attached text is selected, it is surrounded by small white handles, indicating that the text cannot be moved (see fig. 8.16).

Adding Unattached Text

The preceding example explained how to attach text to certain points on a chart. The attached text is fixed to the chosen point and cannot be moved. Some charting situations may require you to include text that you can move and position on the chart. For example, you may want to position text in the form of a brief note or label to explain a specific point on the chart. If you want to include text on a chart that is not attached and can be moved, follow these steps:

8

1. Click the Text tool on the Chart Toolbar. The text you type appears in the formula bar as you enter it. For example, type **3RD QTR. SALES WERE LOWER THAN EXPECTED**.

2. Click the check mark box in the formula bar, or press ⏎Enter.

The unattached text is surrounded by small black handles (see fig. 8.17). You can move the text anywhere on the chart.

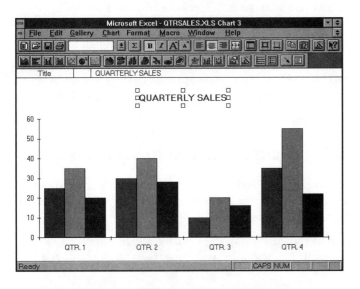

Fig. 8.16
Selected attached text.

8

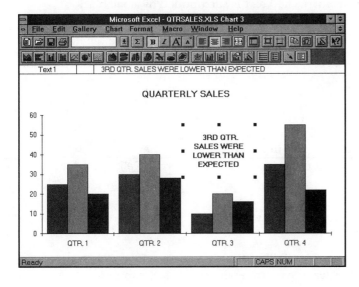

Fig. 8.17
Selected unattached text.

Exercise 2.1: Adding Attached Text to Your Chart

In this exercise, you add a chart title (which is attached text) to your chart in the QTRSALES.XLS worksheet.

1. Open the Chart menu, and choose the Attach Text command. The Attach Text dialog box appears (see fig. 8.15).

2. Select the type of text you want to add. Because you want to add a chart title and that option is already selected, go on to step 3.

3. Choose OK or press ⏎Enter to clear the dialog box and attach text to the chart.

4. Type **ANNUAL SALES**. (The text you type appears in the formula bar.) Then press ⏎Enter. The attached text is surrounded by small white handles.

Exercise 2.2: Adding Unattached Text to Your Chart

In this exercise, you add unattached text to your chart. First, you must deselect the title you just entered in Exercise 2.1 by pressing Esc. When the text is deselected, the white handles disappear.

1. Click the Text tool on the far right of the Chart Toolbar. Type **Model B is doing well**. The text you type appears in the formula bar as you enter it.

2. Press ⏎Enter. The unattached text is surrounded by small black handles.

You can move the text anywhere on the chart by clicking inside the unattached text, holding down the left mouse button, dragging, and then releasing the left mouse button.

Deleting Text

If you want to delete attached or unattached text, use the mouse to select the attached or unattached text on the chart, and then press Del. The selected text disappears.

Formatting Text

You can format text by changing alignment, orientation, font, point size, or style, or by adding a border or pattern. Follow these steps to format text:

1. Select the text you want to format by clicking it with the mouse. The selected text is surrounded by square handles.

2. Open the Format menu, and choose the Text command. The Text dialog box appears (see fig. 8.18).

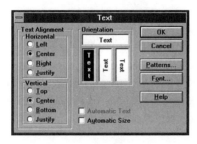

Fig. 8.18
The Text dialog box.

3. Choose from among the Horizontal and Vertical alignments to position the text within its text border. The text can be centered, left-aligned, right-aligned, or justified within the area containing the text.

4. Choose the Orientation style you want from among the text orientation choices. You can rotate selected text to a vertical or sideways orientation. If the selection is too long to display vertically, the text wraps to additional columns.

5. For unattached text, select the Automatic Size check box if you want the border to fit exactly around the text and automatically adjust when the text is changed. Automatic Size is turned off if you resize the area of the unattached text. If you want the text border size to remain fixed, keep Automatic Size turned off.

   If the selected text is attached text, such as a chart title or data series marker, the Automatic Size check box appears dimmed because the attached text area cannot be resized.

   The Automatic Text check box is available only when attached text is selected. This check box enables you to restore attached text to the default text.

6. Choose the Patterns button if you want to access the Format Patterns dialog box and select border and area patterns to apply to the selected area.

7. Choose the Font button if you want to access the Format Font dialog box and change the font, point size, and style of the selected text.

8. Choose OK or press ↵Enter to clear the dialog box and apply the text formatting.

Adding a Pattern and Border to Text

You can add a background pattern and border to selected text to enhance its appearance. The Patterns dialog box appears whenever you double-click a chart object.

The Patterns dialog box is divided into two sections. The Border section on the left side controls the type of border applied to the selected object. The Area section on the right side controls the area inside the border. The options available in both sections include Automatic, None, and Custom. Custom enables you to select from three drop-down lists specific formatting options you can apply to either the border or the area inside the border.

To format text with patterns and a border, follow these steps:

1. Double-click the text you want to format. Or select the text, and then choose the Format Patterns command. The Patterns dialog box appears (see fig. 8.19).

8

Fig. 8.19
The Patterns
dialog box.

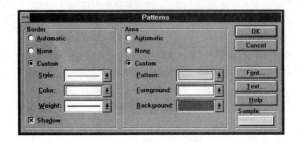

2. Select the Border style you want from the options on the left side of the dialog box. The options are described in table 8.4.

3. Select the Background, Foreground, and Pattern options you want from the drop-down lists on the right side of the dialog box. The options are described in table 8.4.

4. Choose OK or press ↵Enter to clear the dialog box and apply the formatting.

Table 8.4	Patterns Dialog Box Options
Option	*Function*
Automatic (Border)	Applies default border settings
Automatic (Area)	Applies default area settings

Option	Function
None (Border)	Makes border invisible
None (Area)	Makes inside area invisible
Border Style	Controls the style of the line or border; enables you to choose from styles including solid lines, dotted lines, and pattern lines
Border Color	Controls the color of the line or border; enables you to choose from a palette of colors
Border Weight	Controls the thickness of the line or border; enables you to choose a fine line or a thick line
Area Pattern	Controls the pattern inside the selected area; enables you to choose from a list of patterns
Area Foreground	Controls the foreground color of the pattern or fills the selected object with a solid color if a pattern is not chosen; enables you to choose from a palette of colors
Area Background	Controls the background color of the pattern or fills the selected object with a solid color if a pattern is not chosen; enables you to choose from a palette of colors
Shadow	Shadows the background of the border

8

Exercise 2.3: Adding a Pattern and Border to Text

In this exercise, you format the unattached text you added to the chart in Exercise 2.2.

1. Make sure that the unattached text is selected. Black selection handles should appear around the text.
2. Open the Format menu, and choose the Patterns command. The Patterns dialog box appears (see fig. 8.19).
3. Click the Automatic option button in the Border section.

4. Click the down arrow to the right of the Pattern list box to display the Pattern options. From the drop-down list, select the fifth pattern up from the bottom of the list.

5. Choose OK or press ⏎Enter to clear the dialog box and apply the border and pattern.

Selecting Fonts

In the Font dialog box, you can choose from among installed screen fonts and printer fonts. The Font list in the dialog box includes a number of fonts and a Size list with point sizes corresponding to each font type. You also can choose a style for a font, such as bold, italic, or underline; or you can apply formatting commands—such as bold, italics, alignment, and font sizing—using tools on the Standard Toolbar.

To format selected text by changing the font, follow these steps:

1. Select the text you want to format.

2. Open the Format menu, and choose the Font command. The Font dialog box appears (see fig. 8.20).

3. Choose the Font, Size, Font Style, Effects, Color, Background, and other formatting options available in the dialog box. You can see what your selected options will look like in the Sample area.

4. Select the Patterns button if you want to access the Patterns dialog box. Use the Patterns option to apply a border and patterns to the inside area of the selected object.

5. Select the Text button if you want to access the Text dialog box. The Text option controls text alignment and orientation.

6. Choose OK or press ⏎Enter to clear the dialog box and apply the selected formatting.

Fig. 8.20
The Font dialog box.

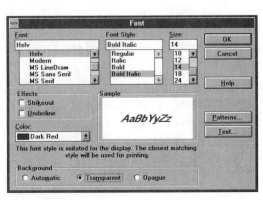

Exercise 2.4: Changing the Font

In this exercise, you change the font of the chart title you created in
Exercise 2.1.

1. Select the title.
2. Open the Format menu, and choose the Font command. The Font
   dialog box appears (see fig. 8.20).
3. Select Bold Italic from the Font Style list box.
4. Select 18 from the Size list box.
5. In the Effects area, select the Underline check box. Notice the new
   appearance of your text in the Sample area.
6. Choose OK or press ⏎Enter to apply the changes to the title of your
   chart.

Adding a Legend

A *legend* is used to identify the data in a chart. Legends usually are necessary
for understanding the way the data is presented. In the section on creating a
chart, you learned that the labels on the horizontal (X) axis are created using
the data from the long side of the selected data. A legend is created from the
short side of the selected data. The legend in fig. 8.21 is created from the short
side of the selected data in the worksheet.

To add a legend to a chart, choose the Legend tool on the Chart Toolbar, or
choose the Chart menu and select the Add Legend command. The legend
appears on the right side of the chart. After you have added a legend to a
chart, the Chart menu command changes to Delete Legend. A chart can have
only one legend.

Moving a Legend

When the legend is selected, it is enclosed by small black handles indicating
that the legend can be moved. To move the legend to another location on the
chart, position the mouse pointer on the legend, press and hold down the left
mouse button, and drag the legend to the desired location. Then release the
mouse button.

8

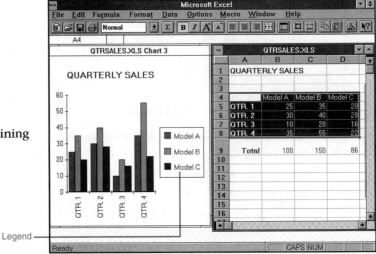

Fig. 8.21
A chart containing
a legend.

Formatting a Legend

8

You can move a legend on a chart with the mouse. You also can use the
Legend dialog box to move and format a legend.

To change the position of a legend, follow these steps:

1. Select the legend by clicking it, or by pressing ⬆ or ⬇ until the
   legend is enclosed by small black handles.

2. Open the Format menu, and choose the Legend command. The
   Legend dialog box appears (see fig. 8.22).

Fig. 8.22
The Legend
dialog box.

3. Choose the Bottom, Corner, Top, Right, or Left position.

4. Choose the Patterns button if you want to access the Patterns dialog
   box. Then choose from among the formatting options.

5. Choose the Font button if you want to access the Font dialog box, and
   select from among the formatting options.

212

6. Choose OK or press ⏎Enter to clear the dialog box and apply the selected formatting.

As with most chart objects, double-clicking the legend displays the Patterns dialog box.

Exercise 2.5: Adding and Formatting a Legend

In this exercise, you add a legend to your chart and change the legend's formatting. Before you begin, make your chart as large as possible by clicking the Maximize button in the separate chart window. If you are using an embedded chart, drag the sizing handles to increase its size.

1. Open the Chart menu, and choose the Add Legend command. The legend appears (with selection handles) on the chart.
2. Open the Format menu, and choose the Legend command. The Legend dialog box appears.
3. Choose the Font button. The Font dialog box appears.
4. Select Italic from the Font Style list box.
5. Choose OK or press ⏎Enter to apply the formatting.

8

Adding Gridlines

You can add gridlines to a chart to help identify the value of a chart marker. Use the Chart Gridlines command to create horizontal or vertical gridlines.

To add major gridlines to a chart, follow these steps:

1. Open the Chart menu, and choose the Gridlines command. The Gridlines dialog box appears (see fig. 8.23).

Fig. 8.23
The Gridlines
dialog box.

2. Select the type of gridlines you want to appear on the chart.

Choose Category (X) Axis gridlines if you want the gridlines to start from the horizontal (X) axis and extend vertically.

213

Choose Value (Y) Axis gridlines if you want the gridlines to start from the vertical (Y) axis and extend horizontally.

If you are adding gridlines to a 3-D chart, the Z-axis gridlines options are available.

3. Choose OK or press ⏎Enter.

After you have added gridlines to a chart, you can format the lines. To format gridlines, follow these steps:

1. Double-click one of the gridlines. Or select a line and choose the Format Patterns command. The Patterns dialog box appears. Choose a line style, color, and weight.

2. Choose OK or press ⏎Enter to clear the Patterns dialog box and apply the selected formatting.

Exercise 2.6: Adding Gridlines

In this exercise, you add horizontal gridlines to your chart in the QTRSALES.XLS worksheet.

1. Open the Chart menu, and choose the Gridlines command. The Gridlines dialog box appears (see fig. 8.23).

2. Select the Major Gridlines check box in the Value (Y) Axis section.

3. Choose OK or press ⏎Enter to place horizontal gridlines in the chart.

Changing the Main Chart Type

Earlier in this chapter you were introduced to the Chart Gallery. The Chart Gallery enables you to change to another chart type. If you have added formatting to a chart and decide that you want to change to another chart type, Excel removes all formatting when you select another chart type. If you want to change to another chart type and preserve your formatting, use the Format Main Chart command.

To change the main chart type and preserve your formatting, follow these steps:

1. Open the Format menu, and choose the Main Chart command. The Format Chart dialog box appears (see fig. 8.24).

2. Select the chart type you want from the Main Chart Type drop-down list.

8

214

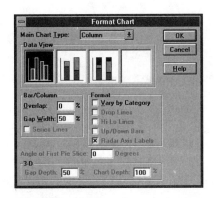

Fig. 8.24
The Format Chart
dialog box.

3. Select other chart formatting from the dialog box. The available formatting options will vary depending on the type of chart selected.

4. Choose OK or press ⏎Enter when you have completed your selections.

Exercise 2.7: Changing the Main Chart Type

In this exercise, you change the main chart type and preserve your formatting.

1. Open the Format menu, and choose the **M**ain Chart command. The Format Chart dialog box appears (see fig. 8.24).

2. Select the Line chart type from the Main Chart **T**ype drop-down list.

3. Choose OK or press ⏎Enter when you have completed your selections.

Copying a Chart to the Clipboard

The Clipboard is used to copy information from one application and place it in another application. Because all Windows applications support the Clipboard, you will find sharing information with other applications easy. The commands for copying information to the Clipboard and extracting the copied information from the Clipboard are the same in all Windows applications. Some non-Windows applications also support extracting information from the Clipboard. Refer to the non-Windows application's documentation for procedures to extract data from the Clipboard.

215

The Clipboard is described in detail in Chapter 4, "Building a Worksheet." You may want to refer to Chapter 4 if you are not familiar with the Clipboard. To copy a chart to the Clipboard, follow these steps:

1. Select the entire chart by clicking anywhere outside the chart plot area. Or open the Chart menu, and choose the Select Chart command. The chart appears enclosed by small white handles when it is selected.

2. Open the Edit menu, and choose the Copy command. A marquee appears around the chart, indicating that the chart has been copied to the Clipboard.

3. Activate the application in which you want to place a copy of the chart.

4. If you are using a Windows application, open the Edit menu, and choose the Paste command. The chart appears in the application.

If you are using a non-Windows application, refer to the application's documentation for the procedures to extract information from the Clipboard.

Objective 3: To Print a Chart

To print an embedded chart, simply print the worksheet in which the chart is embedded. Printing a separate chart is not much different from printing a worksheet. You do not, however, have to define a print area when you print a chart document.

To print a chart displayed in its own document window, follow these steps:

1. Open the File menu, and choose the Page Setup command. The Page Setup dialog box appears (see fig. 8.25).

Fig. 8.25
The Page Setup
dialog box.

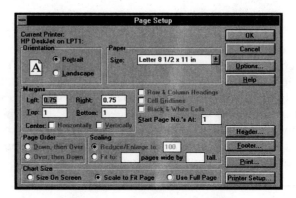

2. Select a Chart Size option. The Size on Screen option prints the chart the same size as it is on-screen. The Scale to Fit Page option prints the chart as large as possible while retaining the height-to-width ratio. The Use Full Page option prints the chart to fit the page, adjusting the height-to-width ratio as necessary.

3. Choose OK or press ⏎Enter when you have completed your selections in the Page Setup dialog box.

4. Open the File menu, and choose the Print Preview command if you want to view the chart in Preview mode before it is printed.

5. Open the File menu, and choose the Print command. The Print dialog box appears.

6. Choose OK or press ⏎Enter to accept the settings and begin printing the chart document.

The printing commands, including Page Setup, Headers and Footers, and Print Preview, are discussed in greater detail in Chapter 7.

Exercise 3.1: Printing a Chart

In this exercise, you print your chart in the QTRSALES.XLS worksheet, using Excel's standard page setup. Before you can begin, you need to have a chart displayed in a separate document window. If you are using an embedded chart, double-click inside the chart to place the chart in a separate window. Click the Maximize button in the chart's window if the window is not already at maximum size.

1. Open the File menu, and choose the Print command. The Print dialog box appears.

2. Choose OK or press ⏎Enter to begin printing.

Summary

In this chapter, you were introduced to many components of charting. This chapter covered topics related to creating and formatting a chart. You learned how to create a chart in a separate chart window, and you learned how to create a chart on a worksheet. This chapter explained how to add titles, legends, attached text, unattached text, and gridlines to enhance the appearance of a chart. You learned how to format chart objects using the formatting commands and various dialog boxes.

8

Charting is a very extensive feature in Excel. This chapter focused primarily on charting basics. If you want to explore charting in more depth and experiment with some of Excel's advanced charting features, you may want to read Que's book *Using Excel 4 for Windows*, Special Edition.

Testing Your Knowledge

True/False Questions

1. The ChartWizard creates charts that are embedded in the worksheet.
2. If your worksheet data selection is taller than it is wide, the labels in the leftmost column of the selection will, by default, appear on a chart's Y-axis.
3. An embedded chart cannot be moved around on a worksheet.
4. When you change the data in a worksheet, a chart embedded in the worksheet will also change to show the new data.
5. When you have selected an embedded chart, clicking and dragging a black handle changes the size of the chart.

Multiple Choice Questions

1. When you double-click a chart object, the _____ dialog box appears.
   - A. Arrow
   - B. Patterns
   - C. Legend
   - D. ChartWizard
2. To change the type of chart displayed in a window, you select a new chart type from the _____ menu.
   - A. Chart
   - B. Format
   - C. Gallery
   - D. none of these answers

8

3. The default chart type is a 2-D _____ chart.

    A. bar

    B. column

    C. line

    D. pie

4. Which of the following are examples of unattached text?

    A. a chart title

    B. a value axis title

    C. a category axis title

    D. none of these answers

5. Which dialog box enables you to control the type of border applied to a selected chart object?

    A. Format

    B. Patterns

    C. Text

    D. none of these answers

Fill-in-the-Blank Questions

1. By default, Excel uses the data along the _____ side of your selection as labels for the X-axis.

2. Text in a chart can be formatted by using the _____ command in the Format menu.

3. By default, Excel uses data along the short side of the selected data in your worksheet to create the _____.

4. The three ways to create a chart in Excel are by using the _____, using the _____, and using the _____.

5. To select nonadjoining areas in your worksheet, you use both the mouse and the _____ key.

Review: Short Projects

1. Creating an Area Chart

    Use the QTRSALES.XLS worksheet to create an area chart that shows sales for Models A, B, and C for the four quarters. The X-axis should be labeled with the data in cells A5 to A8 of the worksheet. The data

219

series should be taken from columns B, C, and D of the worksheet. Include a legend, and print the chart.

2. Creating a Line Chart

Open the Calories worksheet (C3LP1.XLS) you created in the first long project at the end of Chapter 3.

Create a separate line chart with a legend and the chart title CALORIE CONSUMPTION. The chart should have the days of the week on the X-axis and three lines—one each for Breakfast, Lunch, and Dinner. Save the chart on a disk, and then print the chart.

3. Creating a 3-D Pie Chart from Nonadjoining Ranges

Using the ChartWizard, create a 3-D embedded pie chart that shows the percentages of the total calories for each of the days of the week. The embedded chart should have a height of 14 rows and a width of 7 columns. Create an unattached text box that contains your name. Select the worksheet and print it.

Review: Long Projects

1. Creating and Formatting a Chart

Open the NSCC QUARTERLY REPORT worksheet (C4LP1.XLS) you created in the first long project at the end of Chapter 4.

Create a column chart with the four names of the month on the X-axis. The chart should have a set of columns for the Total Expenses data, and a set of columns for the Sales data. For each of the four individual months, the chart should have four columns to represent Sales, and four columns to represent Total Expenses. Add a chart title, legend, and unattached text (your name). Use as many of the different formatting options as you can to change the default text. Include patterns and borders for the text. Spell check your chart. Finally, save and print your chart.

2. Creating a Chart with the Alternative to Excel's Default Layout

Open the worksheet (C4LP2.XLS) you created in the second long project at the end of Chapter 4. Delete the blank row 6.

Create a column chart using the Sales, Income, and Assets data for all eight countries. This chart should have the country names as labels on the X-axis. This is the default chart. Add a formatted title and legend. Add your name as unattached text. Save and print this chart.

Now create a column chart using the same data but use the alternative layout. In this chart, the X-axis labels should be SALES, INCOME, and ASSETS. Add a title and a legend. Add your name as unattached text. Save and print your chart. How are the two charts you printed different?

8

Managing Data

With Excel, you can easily enter, edit, find, and extract database information. After the information in your worksheet is organized into a database, you can use database commands to locate data that meets certain criteria. You can sort a database to put data into a specific order, and you can extract, summarize, and compare data.

This chapter describes what a database is and how to create a database, including how to enter data using a Data Form. This chapter also explains how to define a database range, criteria range, and extract range. You will learn how to sort a database, search for records meeting a specified criteria, and extract records from a database that meet a specified criteria.

Objectives

1. To Understand What a Database Is
2. To Build a Database
3. To Add Records
4. To Delete Records
5. To Sort Records
6. To Search for Records

Key Terms in This Chapter	
Database	A range of cells in a worksheet consisting of a row of field names followed by rows of data records
Record	A row of cells containing fields of related information in a database
Fields	Columns in a database; each column contains one type of information.
Field names	Labels in the first row of a database that identify the contents of a column in a database
Data Form	A form that displays field names, text boxes, and buttons for adding, deleting, and finding records
Criteria	A test condition used to find records in a database
Criteria range	A defined range that includes one or more field names plus at least one row for specified criteria
Extract range	A range that includes field names plus cells to contain extracted records copied from the database

9

Objective 1: To Understand What a Database Is

A *database* stores information in an organized way. A telephone directory is an example of a database. Each individual entry in a telephone directory is a record. Each record has a person's last name, followed by a first name or initial, followed by an address, followed by a phone number. In Excel, you construct a database from a worksheet. Excel databases containing thousands of records are not uncommon. In this chapter you will use a small database.

A row in a database represents a *record*. A record contains related information. The information on each line in a telephone directory, for example, is related because the information refers to the same person or organization.

The records in a database all contain the same *fields*. Each column in a database represents a field. The fields in a database identify the items of information that are required in each record. The first row of a database must contain labels that identify what the database fields are. These labels are referred to as *field names*. Each field name is entered in a separate column in the top row of the database. In a telephone directory database, the field names would be Last Name, First Name, Street, and Phone (see fig. 9.1).

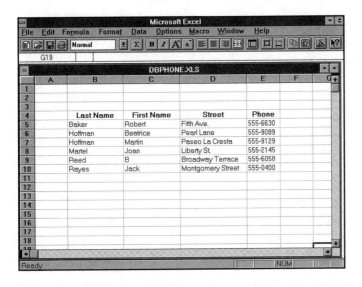

Fig. 9.1
A telephone directory data-base.

To summarize, a database consists of field names and records. You enter individual records in a worksheet row. Each worksheet column in a database has, in its top row, a unique field name that describes the type of information contained in that field in each of the records. Data records immediately follow the field names. After you have entered all the data records, you select the range containing the field names and records and define them as a database. After you have defined the database, you use Excel's database commands to search, sort, and extract the data in the database.

Objective 2: To Build a Database

When you create a database in a worksheet, you must follow some guidelines. You need to consider where you will position the database, for example. A database can fill an entire worksheet; however, if you create a database within an existing worksheet, you must position the database where you can insert additional columns or rows without disturbing the rest of the worksheet. You may need to add additional columns or rows in your database; when a column or row is inserted into a database, the column or row is inserted through the entire worksheet. The same rule applies to the deletion of database rows and columns.

The first row of the database must contain the field names. The field names identify the categories of information required in each record. A field name can consist of up to 255 characters, but you should keep field names brief. Field names must include text, not numbers. (If a field name contains a number, the entire field name must be enclosed in quotation marks for Excel to interpret the name as text.) A field name in a database must be unique—you cannot have two fields with the same field name.

Enter records starting in the first row below the field names. Records can include text, numbers, formulas, and functions. Every record must have the same fields, but you do not have to enter data into all the fields for every record.

In fig. 9.2, the field names in the database, INVOICE, DATE, COMPANY, DUE DATE, and AMOUNT, are entered in row 5. Five records have been entered in rows 6 through 10. The data entered in the records includes dates, text, numbers, and formulas. The formula takes the DATE field in column C and adds 30 days to calculate the DUE DATE.

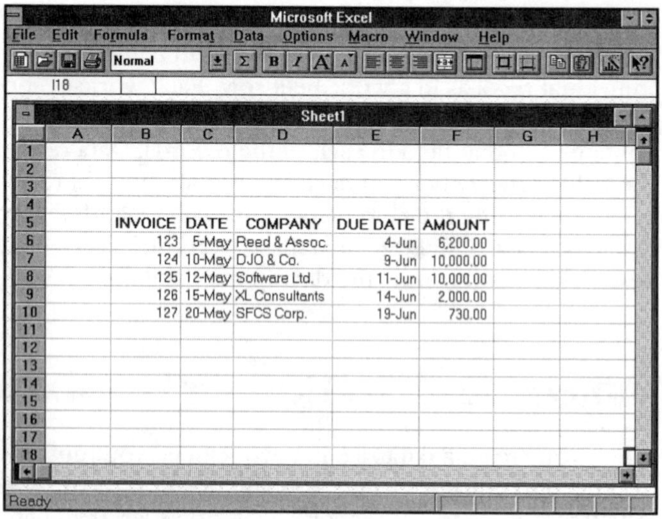

9

Fig. 9.2
A database of
outstanding
invoices.

To begin building a database, enter the field names in the section of the worksheet where you want to start the database. A database can appear in any section of a worksheet. Field names can be entered in two rows to accommodate smaller column widths. However, only the bottom cell is used as the database name.

The field names define the information needed for each record. After you enter field names in the first row, you can begin to enter records.

Exercise 2.1: Entering Field Names and Records

For the exercises in this chapter, you use the data shown in fig. 9.2 in a new worksheet. To enter the field names and records, follow these steps:

1. Enter the field names and data in your worksheet as shown in fig. 9.2. Enter the contents of the DATE field as shown. For example, type **5-May** in cell C6 and press ⏎Enter.

   The DUE DATE field contains a formula that adds 30 days to the corresponding DATE field. In cell E6, enter the formula =C6+30.

2. Save the worksheet on your disk as FIG93.XLS.

Defining a Database

After you have entered the field names and the records, you select the row of field names and the records, and then define the selection as a database. After the database is defined, Excel refers to the data in the selected area when you issue a database command. Excel includes special database commands, such as Find and Extract. These commands work only after you have defined a database. If you have not defined a database and you select a database command, a dialog box displays the message Database range is not defined.

To define a database, follow these steps:

1. Select the row of field names and all the records.

2. Open the Data menu, and choose the Set Database command. Excel names the selected range Database.

Exercise 2.2: Defining Your Database

In this exercise, you define a range of cells as a database. Use the worksheet you created in Exercise 2.1.

1. Select the range of cells from B5 to F10.

2. Open the Data menu, and choose the Set Database command. The word Database appears in the left side of the formula bar.

9

Objective 3: To Add Records

Excel offers two methods for adding records to a database. You can add records into blank cells or rows as you usually do in a worksheet. If you use this method, remember to insert the records within the defined database range. You also can use the **Data Form** method to enter new records into a defined database. The data-entry form presents an organized view of the data and makes data entry easier and more accurate; this method is highly recommended.

Adding a New Record Using the Data Form

After you define a database with the **D**ata Set Data**b**ase command, you can use the Data Form to enter data. To enter data using the Data Form, follow these steps:

1. Open the **D**ata menu, and choose the **F**orm command. The Data Form appears (see fig. 9.3). The Data Form is a dialog box that contains the data for the first record in the database. The Data Form displays the field names in the database; a text box appears to the right of each field name.

9

Fig. 9.3
The Data Form.

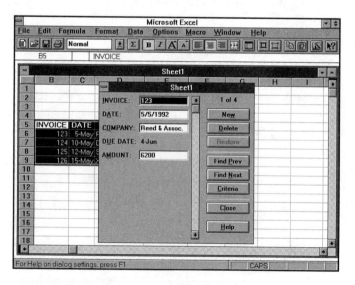

2. To add a new record to the database, choose the New button. A blank form appears, assigning the next record number. New records are added to the end of the database.

3. Enter data for the new record into each text box. Press `Tab⇄` to move forward to the next text box. Press `⇧Shift`+`Tab⇄` to move backward to the preceding text box.

4. Press `↵Enter` after you have entered the data. Another blank form appears, enabling you to enter another new record.

5. Choose the Close button to clear the form and return to the worksheet.

When you use a formula in a database (such as the formula that calculates Due Date in the sample database), you must first enter the formula in the worksheet. You cannot use the Data Form to enter or edit a formula. After you set the database and choose the **Data Form** command, any field containing a formula will appear in the Data Form as a fixed entry; the field name will not have a text box next to it. When you add a new record to the database using the **Data Form New** command, the field containing the formula is automatically calculated when you enter the new record. In fig. 9.3, the DUE DATE field is a fixed entry on the Data Form because the field contains a formula. Excel will enter it for you.

Exercise 3.1: Adding a Record Using the Data Form

9

In this exercise, you use the Data Form to add a record to the database you defined in Exercise 2.2.

1. Open the Data menu, and choose the Form command. The Data Form containing data for your first record appears.

2. Choose the New button. A new record Data Form appears.

3. Enter 128 in the INVOICE field, and press `Tab⇄` to move to the DATE field.

4. Enter 25-May in the DATE field, Becker's Inc., in the COMPANY field, and 200 in the AMOUNT field.

5. Choose the Close button to clear the form and add the record to your database.

You will use this database in a later exercise. Save the database as FIG93.XLS on your disk now.

Objective 4: To Delete Records

You can edit a database using the Data Form, or you can edit directly on the worksheet. When deleting database records, the Data Form is usually the easiest and most accurate method. When you use the form, however, you are limited to deleting one record at a time. The worksheet method enables you to select more than one record to delete. You may inadvertently, however, select a record you do not want to delete. The following steps explain how to delete a record using the form and how to delete a record using the worksheet method.

Deleting a Record Using the Data Form

To delete a record using the Data Form, follow these steps:

1. Open the Data menu, and choose the Form command. The Data Form appears.
2. Choose the Find Next or Find Prev button, or press ⬆ or ⬇ to move to the record you want to delete.
3. Choose the Delete button when the record you want to delete appears on-screen. The records below the deleted record will be renumbered to account for the deleted record. A dialog box appears to remind you that the displayed record will be deleted permanently.
4. Choose OK or press ⏎Enter to delete the record, or select Cancel to keep the record. The warning dialog box disappears.
5. Choose the Close button to return to the worksheet.

Exercise 4.1: Deleting a Record Using the Data Form

In this exercise, you use the Data Form to delete a record. Use the database (FIG93.XLS) you defined in Exercise 2.2.

1. Open the Data menu, and choose the Form command. The Data Form appears.
2. Choose the Find Next button until the record for INVOICE 126 appears on-screen.
3. Choose the Delete button. A dialog box appears to remind you that the displayed record will be deleted permanently.

9

4. Choose OK or press ⏎Enter to delete the record. The warning dialog box disappears.

5. Choose the Close button to return to the worksheet.

Deleting a Record Using the Worksheet Method

To delete a record using the worksheet method, follow these steps:

1. Select the cells containing the record you want to delete. Be sure to select all cells included in the record.

2. Open the Edit menu, and choose the Delete command. The Delete dialog box appears (see fig. 9.4).

Fig. 9.4
The Delete dialog box.

3. Select the Shift Cells Up option.

4. Choose OK or press ⏎Enter. The records below the deleted cells will move up to fill the empty space.

You also can delete an entire row, if you are certain that other data in the worksheet will not be affected by the row deletion.

9

Exercise 4.2: Deleting a Record Using the Worksheet Method

In this exercise, you delete the record for INVOICE 127 from the worksheet.

1. Select the range of cells from B9 to F9.

2. Open the Edit menu, and choose the Delete command. The Delete dialog box appears (see fig. 9.4).

3. Select the Shift Cells Up option, if it is not already selected.

4. Choose OK or press ⏎Enter. The bottom record moves up to row 9.

231

Objective 5: To Sort Records

Excel sorts databases by using fields. Any field name you have created in the database can be used as a sort field for reordering the database. You may, for example, want to sort the records in a telephone directory database according to last name.

When you use Excel's sort capability, you can specify a second sort field and a third sort field, enabling you to perform a sort within a sort. If, for example, you are sorting names in a telephone directory database and several people have the same last name, you can base your second sort on the first name field. If several people have the same last name and the same first name, you can base the third sort on the address.

Make sure that you choose the File Save As command and assign another name to the active document before sorting a database. This command enables you to have two copies of the document. You can work with one copy while the other copy remains intact.

To sort records, follow these steps:

1. Select the records you want to sort. Do not select the database field names. Make sure that you select all columns of each row.

2. Open the Data menu, and choose the Sort command. The Sort dialog box appears (see fig. 9.5).

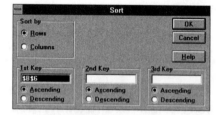

Fig. 9.5
The Sort
dialog box.

3. The 1st Key text box is selected. You must replace the cell address in this text box with the address of any cell in the column that contains the field on which you want to sort. If, for example, you want to sort on the Last Name field and Last Name is in column C, click any cell in column C, or enter a cell address that includes column C as part of the cell address in the text box.

4. Select the Ascending or Descending option for the order in which you want to sort the selected records. The Ascending option sorts the rows

from A to Z. The Descending option reverses this order and sorts from Z to A. Numbers are sorted from the largest negative number to the largest positive number when the Ascending option is selected. Ascending is the default selection.

5. Press ⎡Tab ⎤ or click in the 2nd Key text box if you want to perform a secondary sort within the 1st Key sort. Activate the 3rd Key text box if you want to sort on a third field.

6. Choose OK or press ⎡↵Enter⎤. The selected records are sorted according to the selected options in the Sort dialog box.

If you perform a sort that is incorrect, choose the Edit Undo Sort command to reverse the sort and return to the original database list.

One of the most common sorting errors occurs in the selection process. Excel sorts only the selected cells of a record. If you did not select all the records or all the fields within the records, the sort could create a potential disaster. For example, if you perform a sort and you don't select the last column containing the invoice amount, the sorted data will be misaligned with the correct invoice amount. The selected data is reorganized when a sort is performed, while the unselected data remains in its original order. So remember, select all fields and all records.

The Undo command is a safety net. You can use the command to reverse most mistakes. The Undo command remembers only the last action you performed, however. If you do not catch the mistake right away, the Undo command cannot help you. Hopefully, you will catch your mistake before you save the document. If so, you can close the document without saving the changes. Then, you can reopen the document as it existed originally on your disk. If you save the document with a mistake, locate the previous version of the document in a backup copy.

9

Exercise 5.1: Sorting Records in Your Database

In this exercise, you sort records in your database. Before you start, use the File Open command to open the FIG93.XLS file that you stored on your disk in Exercise 3.1. To sort the records so that they appear in order of increasing AMOUNT, follow these steps:

1. Select the range of cells from B6 to F11. These are the cells you will sort.

2. Open the Data menu, and choose the Sort command. The Sort dialog box appears (see fig. 9.5).

3. The 1st Key text box is already selected. Type F6.

4. Ascending is the default selection so you do not need to change this.

5. Because you are sorting only on one field, choose OK or press ⏎Enter⏎. The selected cells are sorted.

Numbering Records Before Sorting

If you are sorting a database and you want the flexibility to return the database to its original order, you can automatically number each record sequentially before you start the sort. After the sort, you can perform a sort on the numbers. The selected records return to their original order.

Excel includes a data series command that simplifies numbering a long list. To number a list of records in a database so that you can return to a previous order, follow these steps:

1. Enter the number 1 in the cell of a column on one side of the database.

2. Select the cell that contains the number plus the cells below through the end of the database (see fig. 9.6). The selected cells will be numbered sequentially, starting with 1.

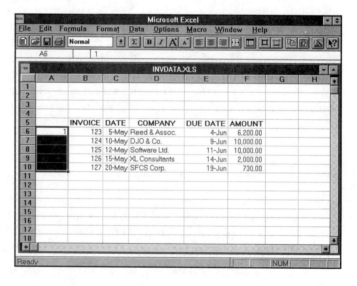

Fig. 9.6
Cells selected for numbering.

3. Open the Data menu, and choose the Series command. The Series dialog box appears (see fig. 9.7).

Fig. 9.7
The Series dialog
box.

4. Choose OK or press ⏎Enter. The default settings in the Series dialog
   box take the first number in the selection and add steps of 1 until
   reaching the end of the selection. The selected cells are numbered
   (see fig. 9.8).

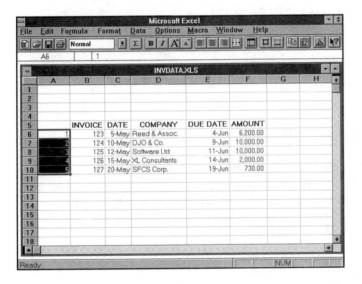

Fig. 9.8
The numbered
cells.

5. Continue sorting the database, using the sorting procedures described
   earlier. Make sure that you include the column containing the numbers in the selection of records to be sorted.

6. To return the records to their original order, select the records to be
   sorted, including the column containing the numbers.

7. Open the Data menu, and choose the Sort command. The Sort dialog
   box appears (see fig. 9.5).

8. Select a cell in the column that contains the numbers. This cell appears as the 1st Key sort.

235

9. Choose OK or press ⏎Enter to clear the dialog box. The selected records are sorted in ascending numerical order, which is the order the records were in originally.

Exercise 5.2: Numbering the Records Using the Data Series Command

In this exercise, you number the records in the FIG93.XLS worksheet so that you can return to a previous order.

1. Enter the number 1 in cell A6.
2. Select the range of cells from A6 to A11. These are the cells you will number.
3. Open the Data menu, and choose the Series command. The Series dialog box appears (see fig. 9.7).
4. Choose OK or press ⏎Enter. The selected cells are numbered.

Objective 6: To Search for Records

9

Sometimes you will want to search a database for records that meet a specified criteria. A *criteria* is a pattern or specific details you are looking for in a record. After you establish criteria, you can use Excel commands to locate records that match the criteria. These commands are extremely useful when you are searching a database that contains many records.

Finding Records

You can define the criteria you want a record to match using the Data Form, or you can define a criteria range on the worksheet and use the Data Find command. The Data Form provides the quickest and easiest method for finding records that satisfy criteria. If you want to find records that match more complex criteria, however, you must define a criteria range on your worksheet and use the Data Find command.

To find records using the Data Form, follow these steps:

1. Open the Data menu, and choose the Form command. The Data Form appears.
2. Choose the Criteria button. A blank Criteria Form appears (see fig. 9.9).

236

Fig. 9.9
A Criteria Form.

3. Select a text box by clicking in it. Enter the criteria or pattern for which you want to search. In fig. 9.10, the search criterion is an amount greater than 2,000. You can enter multiple criteria.

Fig. 9.10
The search criterion.

9

4. Choose the Find Next button after you have entered the criteria. The first record to match the defined criteria appears on-screen. If no matches exist, you hear a beep.

5. Choose the Find Prev button if you want to search backward through the database to find a match.

6. Choose the Close button to clear the dialog box.

Exercise 6.1: Finding a Record Using the Data Form

In this exercise, you find the record with an INVOICE number of 126 in the FIG93.XLS database that you stored on your disk in Exercise 3.1.

1. Open the Data menu, and choose the Form command. The Data Form appears.

2. Choose the Criteria button. A blank Criteria Form appears (see fig. 9.9).

3. Type 126 in the INVOICE text box, which already has the blinking insertion point in it.

4. Choose the Find Next button. The record matching the defined criteria appears on-screen.

5. Choose the Close button to clear the dialog box.

Finding Records Using a Criteria Range

If you want to search for complex or calculated criteria, you should create a criteria range on your worksheet. Defining a criteria range is very similar to defining a database range. A criteria range consists of one or more field names and at least one blank row for entering the criteria.

To define a criteria range, follow these steps:

1. Select the field names you want to use from the row of database field names.

2. Open the Edit menu, and choose the Copy command. Copying the field names from the database field names reduces the chance of error. The field names in the criteria range must match the field names in the database.

3. Select a cell at the beginning of the area you want to use as the criteria range.

4. Open the Edit menu, and choose the Paste command to paste the field names in the top row of the criteria range. In fig. 9.11, field names from the database were copied to the criteria range.

5. Select the pasted field names plus one blank row of cells directly below the criteria field names (see fig. 9.12).

6. Open the Data menu, and choose the Set Criteria command. Excel assigns the name Criteria to the selected range.

Use the blank row below the field names in the criteria range to enter the criteria you want database records to match. The criteria can be simple, such as matching a name, or the criteria can be based on a calculation. After you have entered criteria into the blank cells in the criteria range, you can begin to search the database to find records that match the criteria.

9

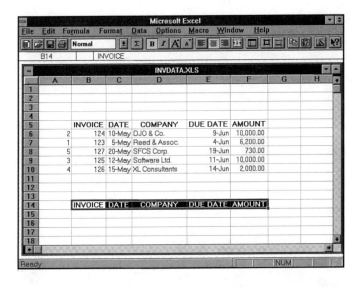

Fig. 9.11
The Field names
copied to the
criteria range.

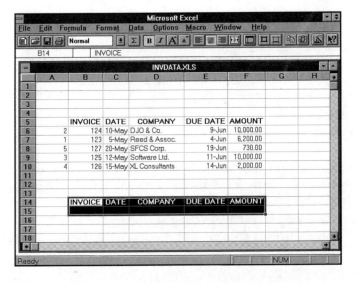

Fig. 9.12
The selected
criteria range.

Suppose, for example, that you want to search an invoice database for records
with a balance due amount of $2,000 or greater. To find the database records
that match the criteria, follow these steps:

1. Enter the criteria >=2000 in the cell directly below the criteria field
   name AMOUNT (see fig. 9.13).

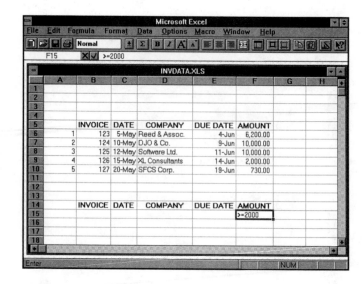

Fig. 9.13
The defined
criteria.

2. Open the Data menu, and choose the Find command. If the active cell was outside the database before the command was selected, the search begins at the top of the database. If the active cell was inside the database, the search begins at the active cell and moves downward. The scroll bars appear with diagonal stripes indicating that the worksheet is in database Find mode.

3. Press ← or → if you want to move the active cell within the selected record. The first record in the database matching the criteria is selected.

4. Click the up or down arrow in the scroll bar area, or press ↑ or ↓ to move forward or backward to the next matching record. If there are no more records that match the criteria, you hear a beep.

5. Open the Data menu, and choose the Exit Find command to return to the normal worksheet mode, or click anywhere outside the database area.

Exercise 6.2: Finding Records Using a Criteria Range

In this exercise, you find the database records that have an AMOUNT field of less than 5,000 in the FIG93.XLS database that you stored on your disk in Exercise 3.1.

240

First, follow these steps to enter the criteria and define the criteria range:

1. Select AMOUNT from the row of database field names.

2. Open the Edit menu, and choose the Copy command.

3. Select cell G13, and press ⏎Enter. Cell G13 now contains AMOUNT.

4. Enter the criteria <5000 in the cell directly below the criteria field name AMOUNT (cell G14).

5. Select cells G13 and G14.

6. Open the Data menu, and choose the Set Criteria command. Criteria appears at the left of the formula bar.

Now follow these steps to find records matching the criteria:

1. Open the Data menu, and choose the Find command. The first record in the database matching the criteria is selected.

2. Click the up or down arrow in the scroll bar, or press ↑ or ↓ to move forward or backward to the next matching record. When there are no more records that match the criteria, you hear a beep.

3. Open the Data menu, and choose the Exit Find command to return to the normal worksheet mode.

Extracting Records from a Database

9

The procedures described in the preceding section enable you to view records that match a specified criteria. In many cases, you will want not only to view the matching records, but also to print or to work with the matching records as a group. Excel enables you to copy records that match the criteria defined in the criteria range to a selected range; the selected range is defined as the extract range.

To set up an extract range, follow these steps:

1. Copy the field names from the database field names to the area you want to use as the extract range. Copying the field names reduces the possibility of error.

2. Select the extract field names and the range below the field names that will contain the copied data. Records will be extracted into the selected area (see fig. 9.14).

3. Open the Data menu, and choose the Set Extract command. The selected range is named Extract.

241

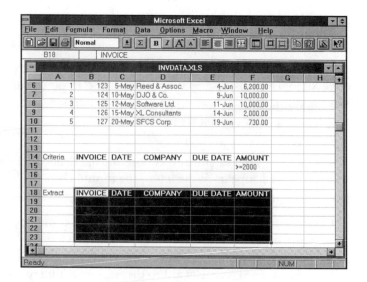

Fig. 9.14
The selected field
names and range.

After the database, criteria, and extract ranges have been set, you can extract data from a database. To extract records, follow these steps:

1. Open the Data menu, and choose the Extract command. The Extract dialog box appears (see fig. 9.15).

Fig. 9.15
The Extract dialog
box.

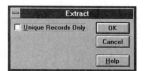

2. If you do not want to extract duplicate records, select the Unique Records Only check box.

3. Choose OK or press ⏎Enter to accept the settings and clear the dialog box. All records in the database that match the criteria are copied to the selected extract range. If the selected range is not large enough to accommodate all matching records, a dialog box appears. Choose OK or press ⏎Enter to clear the dialog box.

You have the option of creating an unlimited extract range that will extract all matching records. To define an unlimited extract range, select only the cells containing the extract field names. If you are using an unlimited extract range, make sure that all cells below the extract field names are clear of data. In the previous database example, the criteria was defined to find or extract all records in the database that have an invoice amount greater than $2000. You also can define multiple criteria in the criteria range on the worksheet or in the Data Form. The following example shows the criteria defined to find all records that are due after June 9 and that have an invoice amount greater than or equal to $2000 (see fig. 9.16).

Fig. 9.16
Multiple criteria
in the Data Form.

The first record that matches the criteria appears (see fig. 9.17). Then the multiple criteria is entered in the criteria range on the worksheet (see fig. 9.18). Finally, Excel copies the records meeting the multiple criteria into the extract range (see fig. 9.19).

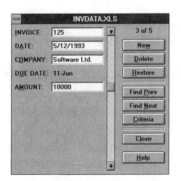

Fig. 9.17
The first match.

9

In addition to defining multiple criteria, you can find or extract records that match one criteria OR another criteria. To find or extract records where one criteria OR the other is met, you must use the criteria range on the worksheet. You cannot use the Data Form if you are looking for records that match one criteria OR the other. To define multiple criteria in the criteria range of the worksheet, you may need to redefine the criteria range. To find or extract records from a database where one criteria OR the other is met, each criteria must be entered in a separate row below the criteria range field names. For example, the defined criteria can look for records that are due after June 9, OR records that have an invoice amount equal to or greater than $2000. Records that match one criteria OR the other are extracted.

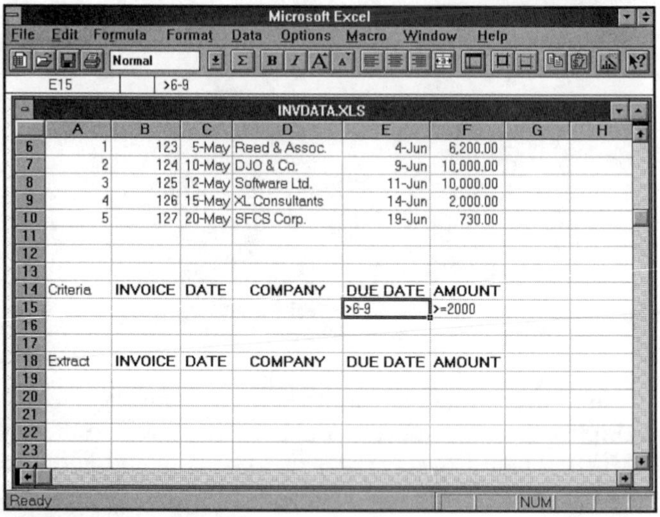

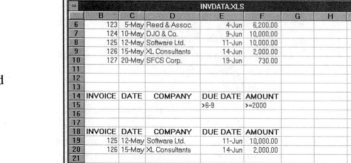

Fig. 9.18
The entered
multiple criteria.

Fig. 9.19
The copied
records.

Exercise 6.3: Extracting Records from the Database

In this exercise, you set up an extract range beginning at row 16 in the FIG93.XLS database that you stored on your disk in Exercise 3.1. Then, you extract records.

To set up the extract range, follow these steps:

1. Copy the field names in cells B5 through F5 into cells B16 through F16.
2. Select the extract field names (B16 through F16). Remember that you can have only one row of field names in the extract range.
3. Open the Data menu, and choose the Set Extract command. Extract appears in the left side of the formula bar.

To extract the records that meet the criteria, follow these steps:

1. Open the Data menu, and choose the Extract command. The Extract dialog box appears (see fig. 9.15).
2. Choose OK or press ⏎Enter to perform the extract and clear the dialog box. All records in the database that match the criteria are copied to the selected extract range.

Summary

9

This chapter introduced you to fundamental database concepts. You learned what a database is and how to create a database on an Excel worksheet. Other topics in the chapter included entering data in a database and using the Data Form to add and delete records. You learned how to set the database range, the criteria range, and the extract range. Additionally, you learned how to define criteria and find records that match the criteria, and you learned how to copy data to an extract range.

If you want to explore databases in more depth and experiment with some of Excel's advanced database features, you may want to read Que's book *Using Excel 4 for Windows*, Special Edition. It includes instructions on how to use Excel's Q+E add-in feature, which enables you to access external databases and bring the data into an Excel worksheet.

Testing Your Knowledge

True/False Questions

1. Each database field name can occupy only one cell.
2. A record is one column in the database.
3. A criteria range will always consist of at least two adjoining cells.
4. The row of field names should be included in the range of cells you are going to sort.
5. When you use the Data Form to insert a record in your database, the database range does not expand to include the new record.

Multiple Choice Questions

1. What command should you use when you first set up the criteria and extract ranges?
    A. Copy
    B. File
    C. Undo
    D. Save As

2. Which menu contains the command that enables you to delete a record from a database?
    A. File
    B. Edit
    C. Tools
    D. none of these answers

3. Which menu contains the command that enables you to define a criteria range?
    A. Edit
    B. Data
    C. Selection
    D. none of these answers

9

4. Excel enables you to sort using up to _____ different fields.

   A. two

   B. three

   C. four

   D. five

5. The range in a worksheet that could consist of just one row is the _____ range.

   A. database

   B. criteria

   C. extract

   D. unique

Fill-in-the-Blank Questions

1. To establish a criteria range to search a database for records with a PAYMENT field value of less than 100, the criteria in the cell under the field name would be _____.

2. The best way to add records to an existing database is by using the Data _____.

3. When you have finished finding records using the Data Find command, you can return to the normal worksheet mode by _____.

4. To find records in a database where one criteria OR the other is met, each criteria must be entered in a separate _____ in the criteria range.

5. The Data _____ command requires only that the database range and the criteria range be set.

Review: Short Projects

Before you start these projects, make sure that the Excel window is maximized so that you can see all the data in your database.

1. Sorting a Database

   Open the C4LP2.XLS file that you created at the end of Chapter 4. Delete row 6 so that the field names are in the row above the data. Save this worksheet on your disk as C9SP1.XLS.

9

Sort the database worksheet in ascending order on the INDUSTRY field, and print the worksheet. Now sort the database in descending order on the NET INCOME field. Then test what happens when you include the row of field names in the sort range and you sort the database on the COUNTRY field. Correct the problem using the Undo Sort command.

If, as you work on this exercise, you find that the Sort dialog box appears over the database so that you can't see the rows and columns to use as sort keys, click the title bar of the dialog box and drag the box to a better position on the screen.

2. Adding Records Using the Data Form

Open the C9SP1.XLS file that you saved at the start of Project 1.

Define cells A5 through H13 as a database. Use the Data Form to add the two records shown in rows 14 and 15 of fig. 9.20. Your worksheet should now look like the one in fig. 9.20. Save the new worksheet as C9SP2.XLS.

9

Fig. 9.20
The completed
Investments
database.

COMPANY	INDUSTRY	COUNTRY	(Mil.) SALES	(Mil.) NET INCOME	(Mil.) ASSETS	(Mil.) MARKET VALUE	PERCENT RETURN ON INVESTED CAPITAL
Solvey	Retail	Australia	11293	273	4262	3939	12.1
Olnza	Machine	Spain	7602	1174	14114	14640	13.9
Nordlund	Optical	Norway	5476	291	5991	1438	9.7
Nobunaga	Steel	Japan	11709	294	16036	8630	4.7
Lucus & Smith	Aerospace	U. K.	8272	160	8964	5415	7.3
Kesko	Diversified	Brazil	6242	715	11684	9554	9.6
Dumez	Electronic	Italy	4283	66	2786	994	7.2
CNX	Automobile	Germany	12579	268	12059	2180	10.8
Metsuhita	Electronic	Japan	7041	295	14923	13876	12.8
PCE Inc.	Optical	USA	9278	220	5062	6294	6.3

3. Finding Records Using the Data Form

Open the C9SP2.XLS file that you saved at the end of Project 2.

Use the Data Form to find all the records of companies in the Automobile industry. Then use the Data Form to find the records of all the companies with a Percent Return on Invested Capital less than 9%.

Review: Long Projects

1. Sorting a Database on Multiple Fields; Using the Criteria Range and Extract Range

Open the C9SP2.XLS database. Sort the database in ascending order. Use the following multiple sort keys:

1st key = COUNTRY   2nd key = INDUSTRY   3rd key = VALUE

Set up a criteria range, and then use the Data Find command to find all the records of companies in the Automobile industry. Then use the Data Find command to find the records of all the companies with a Percent Return on Invested Capital less than 9%.

Set up an extract range, and extract into the range the records of all the companies with a Percent Return on Invested Capital less than 9%. Print the field names and the records in the extract range.

2. Setting Up a Database of Friends and Classmates

Include (at least) the following fields: Last Name, First Name, Initial, Age, Gender, Phone, Birthday

Save the worksheet on your disk, and then use the Data Form to delete and add records. Sort the database so that it is in alphabetical order using the Last Name, First Name, and Initial fields. Use the Data Form to find records. Set up a criteria range to find the records with Smith in the Last Name field OR an Age over 30 (you may need to add some new "friends" to your database first). Extract these records and print them.

9

Summary of Excel 4.0 for Windows Commands

Y ou can use this appendix to look up the commands used in Excel 4.0 for Windows. The following tables provide the keyboard strokes and mouse actions necessary to execute the commands. Each table covers the various activities you can perform in Excel, such as editing a worksheet, formatting a worksheet, and so on.

Using Dialog Boxes

Task	Keyboard	Mouse
Select text box	[Tab⇄] or [Alt]+**underlined letter**	Click text box
Select option button	[Tab⇄],**arrow key**	Click button
Select (deselect) check box	[Tab⇄],**space bar**	Click check box
Choose command	[Alt]+**underlined letter**	Click command button
Choose OK	[↵Enter]	Click OK button
Choose Cancel	[Esc]	Click Cancel button

Moving the Active Cell

Task	Keyboard	Mouse
Move one cell left	[←]	Click cell with cell pointer
Move one cell right	[→]	Click cell with cell pointer
Move one cell up	[↑]	Click cell with cell pointer
Move one cell down	[↓]	Click cell with cell pointer
Move to next block of data separated by a blank cell	[Ctrl]+**arrow key**	Click cell with cell pointer
Move to column A of active row	[Home]	Click cell with cell pointer

A

Task	Keyboard	Mouse
Move to cell A1	Ctrl + Home	Click cell A1 with cell pointer
Move to rightmost column containing data	Ctrl + →	Click cell with cell pointer
Move to last cell used in worksheet	Ctrl + End	Click cell with cell pointer
Move up one full window	PgUp	Click in vertical scroll bar above scroll box
Move down one full window	PgDn	Click in vertical scroll bar below scroll box
Move one screen left	Ctrl + PgUp	Click in horizontal scroll bar left of scroll box
Move one screen right	Ctrl + PgDn	Click in horizontal scroll bar right of scroll box
Move to specified cell or named range	F5	Click Formula menu and choose Goto; enter cell address

A

Editing in the Formula Bar

Task	Keyboard	Mouse
Activate formula bar	F2	Click in formula bar
Move cursor	← or →	Click at desired location in formula bar

continues

253

Task	Keyboard	Mouse
Move cursor to end of line	End	Click at end of formula bar
Move cursor to beginning of line	Home	Click at beginning of line
Delete character to left of cursor	◆Backspace	Select character and press Del
Delete character to right of cursor	Del	Select character and press Del
Accept formula bar entry	↵Enter	Click check mark box
Cancel formula bar entry	Esc	Click X box

Saving, Opening, Closing, and Deleting Files

A

Task	Keyboard	Mouse
Save a file	Alt, F, S, or ⇧Shift + F12	Click File menu and choose Save
Save a copy of a named file	Alt, F, A, or F12	Click File menu and choose Save As
Save a workbook	Alt, F, W	Click File menu and choose Save Workgroup
Save a file to another file format	Alt, F, A, Alt + T, ↑ or ↓	Click File menu, choose Save As, and select file format from Save File As Type list
Close a file	Alt, F, C, or Ctrl + F4	Click File menu and choose Close

254

Task	Keyboard	Mouse
Close all open files	Hold down `⇧Shift`, press `Alt`,`F`,`C`	Hold down `⇧Shift`, click File menu, and choose **Close All**
Delete a file from disk	`Alt`,`F`,`D`	Click **File** menu and choose **Delete**

Working with Ranges

Task	Keyboard	Mouse
Select a range of cells	Hold down `⇧Shift`, or press `F8` to use Extend mode; press **arrow keys** to select range of cells	Drag over range of cells you want to select

Editing a Worksheet

Task	Keyboard	Mouse
Insert blank cells	Select number of cells you want to insert; press `Alt`,`E`,`I`	Select number of cells you want to insert; click **Edit** menu and choose **Insert**
Delete cells	Select cells you want to delete; press `Alt`,`E`,`D`	Select cells you want to delete; click **Edit** menu and choose **Delete**

continues

A

255

Task	Keyboard	Mouse
Insert a blank column	[Ctrl]+**space bar** to select active column; press [Alt],[E],[I]	Click column heading; click **Edit** menu and choose **Insert**
Delete a column	[Ctrl]+**space bar** to select active column; press [Alt],[E],[D]	Click column heading; click **Edit** menu and choose **Delete**
Insert a row	[Shift]+**space bar** to select active row; press [Alt],[E],[I]	Click row heading; click **Edit** menu and choose **Insert**
Delete a row	[Shift]+**space bar** to select active row; press [Alt],[E],[D]	Click row heading; click **Edit** menu and choose **Delete**
Erase cell contents	[Del] or press [Alt],[E],[E]	Click **Edit** menu and choose **Clear**
Copy cell contents to Clipboard	Select cells to be copied; press [Alt],[E],[C] or press [Ctrl]+[C]	Select cells to be copied; click **Edit** menu and choose **Copy**
Paste copied cells	[Alt],[E],[P] or press [Ctrl]+[V]	Click **Edit** menu and choose **Paste**
Copy cell contents to adjacent cells to the right	[Alt],[E],[H] or press [Ctrl]+[R]	Click **Edit** menu and choose **Fill Right**
Copy cell contents to adjacent cells below	[Alt],[E],[W] or press [Ctrl]+[R]	Click **Edit** menu and choose **Fill Down**
Copy cell contents to adjacent cells above	Hold down [Shift]; press [Alt],[E],[W]	Hold down [Shift]; click **Edit** menu and choose **Fill Up** (**w**)

A

Task	Keyboard	Mouse
Copy cell contents to adjacent cells to the left	Hold down ⸢⇧Shift⸣; press ⸢Alt⸣, ⸢E⸣, ⸢H⸣	Hold down ⸢⇧Shift⸣; click **Edit** menu and choose **Fill Left** (**h**)
Move cell contents	Select cells you want to move; press ⸢Alt⸣, ⸢E⸣, ⸢T⸣ or press ⸢Ctrl⸣+⸢X⸣; select cell marking new location; press ⸢Alt⸣, ⸢E⸣, ⸢P⸣, or press ⸢↵Enter⸣ or ⸢Ctrl⸣+⸢V⸣ to move selected data from old location to new	Select cells you want to move; click **Edit** menu and choose **Cut**; select cell marking new location; click **Edit** menu and choose **Paste**
Change column width	⸢Alt⸣, ⸢T⸣, ⸢C⸣	Drag right border of column heading until desired column width is reached
Adjust column width to widest cell in column	⸢Alt⸣, ⸢T⸣, ⸢C⸣, ⸢Alt⸣+⸢B⸣	Double-click right border of the column heading
Change row height	⸢Alt⸣, ⸢T⸣, ⸢R⸣	Drag bottom border of row heading until desired row height is reached
Check Spelling	⸢Alt⸣, ⸢O⸣, ⸢S⸣	Click **Options** menu and choose **Spelling**
Reverse last action	⸢Alt⸣, ⸢E⸣, ⸢U⸣	Click **Edit** menu and choose **Undo**

A

Formatting a Worksheet

Task	Keyboard	Mouse
Format a number	(Alt),(T),(N)	Click Format menu and choose **Number**
Format a date or time	(Alt),(T),(N)	Click Format menu and choose **Number**
Change cell alignment	(Alt),(T),(A)	Click Left, Right, or Center tool on Toolbar, or click Format menu and choose **Alignment**
Make selection bold or italic	(Alt),(T),(F)	Choose Bold or Italic tool on Toolbar, or click Format menu and choose **Font**
Change a font	(Alt),(T),(F)	Click Format menu and choose **Font**
Justify cells to align within a selected range	(Alt),(T),(J)	Click Format menu and choose **Justify**
Add borders to selected cells	(Alt),(T),(B)	Click Format menu and choose **Border**
Add patterns to selected cells	(Alt),(T),(P)	Click Format menu and choose **Patterns**
Add borders and patterns to selected object	(Alt),(T),(P)	Double-click an object, or click Format menu and choose **Patterns**
Create a style based on selected formatting	(Alt),(T),(S), (Alt),(D)	Click Format menu and choose **Style**; choose **Define** button
Apply predefined formatting to range of cells	(Alt),(T),(M)	Click Format menu and choose Autoformat or click Autoformat tool

A

Entering Functions

Task	Keyboard	Mouse
Enter a predefined function into cell or formula	[Alt],[R],[T], or press [⇧Shift]+[F3]	Click Formula menu and choose Paste Function

Printing

Task	Keyboard	Mouse
Select a range to be printed	Hold down [⇧Shift] and press **arrow keys** to select range	Drag over area you want to select
Select nonadjacent ranges	Select first area, press [⇧Shift]+[F8] for Add mode, move to next area using **arrow keys**; hold down [⇧Shift] and press **arrow keys** to add range to selection	Drag over first area you want to select; hold down [Ctrl] and drag over next area
Define area to be printed	[Alt],[O],[A]	Click **Options** menu and choose Set Print **Area**
Add titles to print on every page	[Alt],[O],[T]	Click **Options** menu and choose Set Print **Titles**
Define a page break	[Alt],[O],[B]	Click **Options** menu and choose Set Page **Break**
View document before it prints	[Alt],[F],[V]	Click **File** menu and choose Print **Preview**

continues

A

259

Task	Keyboard	Mouse
Add headers and footers to document	Alt, F, T, Alt + A (header) or Alt + F (footer)	Click File menu and choose Page Setup; click Header button or Footer button
Change page orientation	Alt, F, T, Alt + R (Portrait) or Alt + L (Landscape)	Click File menu and choose Page Setup; select Portrait or Landscape option
Adjust margins	Alt, F, T	Click File menu and choose Page Setup
Switch to another printer or change default settings on the current printer	Alt, F, T, Alt + N	Click File menu, choose Page Setup, and select the Printer Setup button
Print the defined area	Alt, F, P, or Ctrl + Shift + F12	Click File menu and choose Print
Print multiple ranges at one time	Alt, F, E	Click File menu and choose Print Report

A

Charting

Task	Keyboard	Mouse
Create a separate chart document from selected data	F11 or Alt + F1	Click File menu and choose New; select chart from dialog box and choose OK
Change the chart type	Alt, G (select chart type from Gallery menu); select a predefined chart format displayed in dialog box by entering number of chart format	Click Gallery menu on the Chart menu bar, and select a chart type from list; double-click predefined chart format displayed in dialog box

Task	Keyboard	Mouse
Change the pre-ferred chart type	Alt, G, T	Click **Gallery** menu and choose **Set Preferred**
Add a chart title	Alt, C, T	Click **Chart** menu and choose Attach **Text**
Add a chart legend	Alt, C, L	Click **Chart** menu and choose Add **Legend**, or click Legend tool
Format a selected chart object with borders and patterns	Alt, T, P	Double-click chart object you want to format
Add gridlines to chart	Alt, C, G	Click **Chart** menu and choose **Gridlines**; or click Gridlines tool
Modify view of a 3-D chart	Alt, T, 3	Click **Format** menu and choose **3-D View**
Change chart type without losing custom formatting	Alt, T, M	Click **Format** menu and choose **Main Chart**
Change font	Alt, T, F	Click **Format** menu and choose **Font**
Change text orientation or alignment	Alt, T, T	Click **Format** menu and choose **Text**
Check spelling	Alt, C, S	Click **Chart** menu and choose **Spelling**

A

Using a Database

Task	Keyboard	Mouse
Define a database	Select field names and records; press [Alt],[D],[B]	Click **Data** menu and choose Set Data**b**ase
View a database by form	[Alt],[D],[O]	Click **Data** menu and choose **Form**
Add a record to a database form	[Alt],[D],[O], [Alt]+[W]	Click **Data** menu and choose **Form**; choose **New** button
Delete a record from a database form	[Alt],[D],[O], [Alt]+[D]	Click **Data** menu and choose **Form**; choose **Delete** button
Sort selected records	[Alt],[D],[S]	Click **Data** menu and choose **Sort**
Define range for criteria	[Alt],[D],[C]	Click **Data** menu and choose Set **Criteria**
Find records that match criteria	[Alt],[D],[F]	Click **Data** menu and choose **Find**
Define range for extracting records from a database	[Alt],[D],[X]	Click **Data** menu and choose Set **Extract**
Extract records that match the defined criteria from database	[Alt],[D],[E]	Click **Data** menu and choose **Extract**

A

Using On-line Help

Task	Keyboard	Mouse
Access the Help Index	F1	Click **Help** menu and choose **Contents**
Access Lotus 1-2-3 Help	Alt, H, L	Click **Help** menu and choose **Lotus 1-2-3**

Modifying Workspace Settings

Task	Keyboard	Mouse
Display Toolbars	Alt, O, O	Click **Options** menu and choose **Toolbars**
Remove worksheet gridlines	Alt, O, D, Alt + G	Click **Options** menu and choose **Display**; select **Gridlines** check box
Increase or decrease magnification in a worksheet	Alt, W, Z	Click **Window** menu and choose **Zoom**; select or enter the amount of magnification

A

Index

X-Z